MW00883199

THE ONLY RENTAL PROPERTY INVESTING BOOK YOU'LL EVER NEED:

THE ULTIMATE GUIDE TO FINDING, BUYING, & MANAGING RENTAL PROPERTIES USING LONG & SHORT TERM RENTAL INVESTING STRATEGIES

ANDREW & COURTNEY JAMES

PERMANENT
PTO
Spend Life Living

© **Copyright 2024 - All rights reserved.**

The content contained within this book may not be reproduced, duplicated or transmitted without direct written permission from the author or the publisher.

<u>Limit of Liability:</u> Although the author and publisher have made reasonable efforts to ensure that the contents of this book were correct at press time, the author and publisher do not make, and hereby disclaim, any representations and warranties regarding the content of the book, whether express or implied, including implied warranties of merchantability or fitness for a particular purpose. You use the contents in this book at your own risk. Author and publisher herby disclaim any liability to any other party for any loss, damage, or cost arising from or related to the accuracy or completeness of the contents of the book, including any errors or omissions in this book, regardless of the cause. Neither the author nor the publisher shall be held liable or responsible to any person or entity with the respect to any loss or incidental, indirect, or consequential damage caused, or alleged to have been caused, directly or indirectly, by the contents contained herein. The contents of this book are informational in nature and are not legal or tax advice, and the authors and publishers are not engaged in the provision of legal, tax, or any other advice. You should seek your own advice from professional advisors, including lawyers and accountants, regarding the legal, tax, and financial implications of any real estate transaction you contemplate.

<u>Legal Notice:</u>

This book is copyright protected. It is only for personal use. It cannot be amended, distributed, sold, used, quoted or paraphrased any part, or the content within this book, without the consent of the author or publisher.

Published by Read Street Press LLC, Appleton, WI

Copyright © 2024 by Read Street Press LLC

DOWNLOAD THE AUDIOBOOK
VERSION FOR FREE

If you love listening to audiobooks on-the-go, you can download the audiobook version of this book for FREE (Regularly $14.95) just by signing up for a FREE 30-day audible trial!

Visit the link below to get started:
https://bit.ly/rental-investing-acx-us

CONTENTS

INTRODUCTION: WHY I LOVE RENTAL PROPERTY INVESTING

"Don't wait to buy real estate. Buy real estate and wait."

— *WILL ROGERS*

What would you do if you had no boss? No set schedule? No clock to punch or to-do list to complete? What if you had nothing but time?

I used to sit at my desk and ponder those exact questions. What would it be like if I wasn't working for the weekend? If the thought of layoffs and downsizing didn't constantly hang over my head?

I like to call that guy Old Andrew because he feels like a completely different person. That guy had a job that didn't challenge him. He made enough money to cover his bills, but not nearly enough to fund the lifestyle of his dreams. He was looking at the typical American life: 9-to-5, climbing the career ladder, retiring at 65 if everything went according to plan, and having a decade or so of freedom to actually enjoy the fruits of his labor.

Old Andrew was surviving, but he certainly wasn't thriving. His frustration mounted every single time he sat down at his desk. And eventually, he got sick of daydreaming about the life he wanted.

So, he took control. He rented out the second story of his duplex and kickstarted a real estate investing journey that changed his life.

HOW REAL ESTATE INVESTING CHANGED MY LIFE

My shift from Old Andrew to New Andrew—aka, the guy writing this book—began when I met my wife. Her passion for real estate sparked my curiosity and pushed me to dip my toe into house hacking (renting out a room or unit of your personal residence with the goal of lowering your expenses). Before I knew it, I had tenants living in the second story of my duplex. When I cashed that first rent check—enough to cover my mortgage—it felt like the sun was peeking through the clouds.

Could real estate investing be my ticket out of my 9-to-5? It sure felt like it. I learned everything I could about the industry, developed my own blueprint for finding great deals, and adapted my strategy as I became more knowledgeable.

Life looks really, really different now. I don't punch a clock anymore. Instead, I spend my time planning and enjoying trips with my wife. I've seen new countries, indulged in some incredible new cuisines, and checked off a few items on my ever-growing bucket list. I have the house of my dreams with plenty of space to tinker with DIY projects and a kitchen that makes me feel like I'm hosting a show on the Food Network.

Real estate investing changed my life. It can change yours, too.

THE BOOK I WISH I HAD

At its core, real estate investing is very simple. It's a tried-and-true wealth-building strategy because it's straightforward: buy property. Rent it or flip it. Repeat.

Everyone can do it. Not everyone can be great at it. Being a successful real estate investor is due to tons of tiny decisions that add up to massive results. When I started house hacking, I quickly realized I had a lot to learn. My wife helped a lot, but there are some things only experience can teach you. I went from house hacking to owning multiple properties, including commercial rentals. I went from being a hands-on landlord to employing a team to manage my properties so I could live life to the fullest. Each phase had its own set of challenges, opportunities, and benefits. I learned something new at every single turn.

This is the book I wished I had throughout that journey. It probably caught your attention because you're in the same mindset as Old Andrew. You're feeling broke and frustrated, desperate to provide for your family. You're sick of having your earning potential dictated by your boss or corporate politics. You're a go-getter, and you want to go out there and get it: wealth, assets, and most importantly, control of your time and living life on your terms.

Real estate investing can give you this freedom. This book will give you the blueprint you need to get started and scale, especially if you are:

- Overwhelmed by your real estate options and don't know where to start. There are lots of terms, jargon, and strategies you need to learn to be successful. I'll break them down for you to shorten your learning curve.
- Building your empire. Managing one property is tough. Managing multiple properties is even tougher. And managing more than five is insanely tough, especially if you don't have the systems and team.

I've been there, done that. When you're finished with this book, you'll not only feel confident purchasing and managing your first investment property, but you'll be able to manage a second, third, fourth—as many properties as you want—with ease.

In the next pages, you're going to learn:

- How to find incredible deals
- The ins and outs of creative financing, including how to fund deals with little to no money and a poor credit score
- How to build a system to manage your properties that actually works

- Ways to manage short-term, midterm, and vacation rentals
- How to scale and exit when the time is right

Listen, I'm no mogul. I'm a regular guy who put in the work to learn this business and worked the steps I'm going to lay out for you in the chapters to follow. Jumping into real estate investing was a risk, but most worthwhile things are. If you're ready to take the plunge, read on.

HOW RENTAL PROPERTY INVESTING WORKS & HOW IT CAN BUILD YOU WEALTH YOU NEVER IMAGINED

"Ninety percent of all millionaires become so through owning real estate. More money has been made in real estate than in all industrial investments combined. The wise young man or wage earner of today invests his money in real estate."

— *ANDREW CARNEGIE*

"I can't purchase property right now. Interest rates are through the roof."

"I missed the window to invest in property. Best to keep saving and wait until prices come down again."

"I can't risk having a property sit vacant. If I'm not collecting rent, there's no way to make money investing in real estate."

Sound familiar? You're not alone. Lots of people dream of investing in real estate. Many never take the plunge because of thoughts just like the ones above. But most of that fear comes from a lack of knowledge about the industry.

Thankfully, that's easy to fix. In this chapter, you'll get a crash course in real estate investing. We'll go beyond the basics, look at each phase of the real estate cycle, examine four ways investing can make you money, and give you a realistic picture of the pros and cons of starting today instead of in the distant future.

WHY REAL ESTATE INVESTING IS SO POWERFUL

When was the last time you paid rent? Maybe it was a few years ago when you split that four-bedroom house with your buddies from college. Perhaps it was those first few years as a newlywed, renting a tiny house in the city. Maybe it was two weeks ago when you wrote a $1,500 check to your landlord.

Let me tell you what happened to that cash. Your landlord used it to pay the mortgage on the place you live in. While you live in that property and pay their mortgage, the value appreciates, and your landlord racks up tax benefits. They're rolling excess cash flow into new properties.

This is why real estate investing is so powerful. Your hard-earned cash is making your landlord rich. It could be making you rich instead.

THE BIG FOUR: HOW REAL ESTATE CAN MAKE YOU WEALTHY

We all want to make money while we sleep. Real estate investing makes that possible, and there's more than one way to make it happen. Your property can generate value for you in four major ways: appreciation, cash flow, tax benefits, and loan paydowns.

You need just one property to start this process. As value grows, you'll be able to snowball that into more properties and, eventually, more income.

Here's how each of The Big Four elements work:

Appreciation

Let's do a little experiment. Head to Zillow and search for the address of your childhood home. Write down the Zestimate at the top of the page. Then, scroll down to the price history and look at the sale price for the last few times the home was bought and sold.

You'll likely find a pretty big difference between the current projected value and the recent sale prices. That's appreciation in action.

Appreciation refers to the increase of an asset's value over time. It is split into two categories: natural and forced.

Natural appreciation occurs when market forces outside the investor's control, like inflation, economic growth, or population changes, drive an asset's value up. Forced appreciation occurs when the investor makes decisions that increase the property's value. Investors can create forced appreciation by raising rent or making property improvements.

Natural appreciation is ideal because it doesn't require hands-on work from the owner to increase its value. Instead, the time investment is used on the front end of the purchase when you go through a thorough due diligence process to understand the external factors that can impact the property's value. Forced appreciation requires an investment of time and money after purchasing the property, in addition to the time spent researching the investment before purchasing. In an ideal scenario, an investor can find a property that is not only likely to experience natural appreciation, but also offers an opportunity for improvements that lead to forced appreciation.

Cash Flow

In real estate investing, cash flow is exactly what it sounds like: the movement of money in and out of your property. Every property you own should generate income, typically through rental income. Each property will also come with its share of expenses, like mortgage payments, taxes, and operation expenses.

The easiest way to calculate your cash flow will take you right back to basic mathematics. Add up the expenses on the property, then subtract it from the income. The result is your cash flow.

Income - expenses = cash flow

Accurately tracking your cash flow requires diligence because there are hidden expenses to property ownership and management. Repairs, security, access systems, and property maintenance all need to be accounted for when calculating cash flow. As your real estate empire expands and your team grows, you'll have things like property management fees to account for as well.

If your expenses exceed your income, you are experiencing negative cash flow. If expenses and income are equal, you still have negative cash flow. Your goal is to have positive cash flow, which means your income exceeds your expenses. When that happens, give yourself a pat on the back and celebrate—you're making money!

Tax Benefits

As Benjamin Franklin said, the only certainty in life is death and taxes. Let's talk about taxes.

Taxes are an inevitable part of real estate investing or any income-generating activity. Thankfully, some tax benefits to property ownership and real estate investing can lighten your tax burden. When you invest in real estate, you often qualify for pass-through deductions and tax write-offs, among other advantages. Deductions will lower your taxable income. Some deductions, like taxes and mortgage interest, are fairly obvious. Others, like business equipment or travel expenses, are less obvious but can add up to big savings. Some common tax benefits include:

- Subtracting a decrease in property value from your taxable income
- Using a 1031 exchange to defer taxes after selling an investment property and investing in a new property
- Writing off the value of replacing your investment property's HVAC system

These are just a few examples of the tax benefits of real estate investing. A great accountant or tax strategist can help you make the most of your benefits. They'll prove their value over and over again and quickly become crucial players on your team. We'll talk more about how to find these teammates in the next chapter.

Loan Paydown

You will likely take out a loan to finance property purchases. When you have tenants, their rent payments can go directly toward paying down your loan. As you pay down the principal, you grow the equity on your property. Paying off your loan early can save you money on interest and give you more capital to invest in new properties.

UNDERSTANDING RENTAL PROPERTY INVESTING

Real estate investing is a big umbrella. In the broadest sense, it is the act of purchasing a property with the ultimate goal to generate a return. You can do this through residential or commercial properties. We will focus on rental properties throughout this book, but the principles are the same for commercial investing.

There is a big difference between simply buying a house and investing in a rental property. The devil, of course, is in the details.

When you invest in a rental property, you are investing with the ultimate goal of getting a return on your investment, typically through income or appreciation. You might never cook a meal in this residence's kitchen or have a drink on its back porch. Heck, you might not even live in the same city as this residence.

When you purchase a home as your primary residence, you often consider factors unique to your family, like the number of bedrooms or the length of the commute to work. When you invest in rental properties, you become the landlord, and your considerations change. In addition to the property's features like location or size, you also need to consider other factors, like:

- **Maintenance costs:** You are the landlord, which means getting the property move-in ready—and keeping it in that condition—is your responsibility. It's crucial to be honest about whether you can complete the maintenance work yourself or if you have the financial bandwidth to hire someone else to do the work.

- **The desirability for tenants:** It's important to have a clear picture of the potential tenants for the property. Are you offering a long-term rental for families? Mid-term rentals for traveling nurses or other similar professionals? How much work will you have to do to keep the property occupied, and can you handle having the property vacant for a few months between tenants?
- **State and local ordinances:** There are laws and regulations for rental properties, and they often vary by state and location. You'll need to comply with these ordinances and regulations as well as keep up-to-date on changes after you purchase the property.
- **Your own personal finances:** Can this property generate enough income to make the work worthwhile? What is the average rent for similar properties in the area? How much will it cost to insure the property? Have a clear understanding of your personal financial health before you add another property into the mix.

Remember, your goal is not to build a home for yourself. Your goal is to find the right property, fill it with the right tenants, charge them the right price, and use that income to generate more wealth for yourself. To do this successfully, you need a strategy and a plan. Most of all, you need knowledge of how rental property investing works and how to make decisions based on the phase of the real estate cycle you're in.

OTHER PROS OF REAL ESTATE INVESTING

For most of us, myself included, real estate investment is an attractive option because it gives us more control over our income and no cap on our earning potential. There are other benefits to jumping in, as I've discovered since taking the plunge.

Unlock the Power of Leverage

You can start investing in real estate without a ton of capital. When you use leverage, you are using borrowed money or debt to set yourself up for a return on your investment. Through mortgages and other purchasing incentives, you can purchase your first property with very little upfront capital and begin your journey. As your cash flow increases, you'll be able to invest in more properties. Leverage makes real estate an accessible way to grow your wealth and scale your business.

Success Is Dependent on the Person

I won't lie to you: making money through real estate investing takes work, especially in the beginning. The great news is that your success is entirely dependent on you. You have the power to improve your skills and expand your real estate knowledge. You have the power to use your personal time to hunt for deals and vet tenants. You have the power to set big dreams for your business and take action to make them happen. Your ability to succeed is entirely in your hands. Yes, it's hard. Is it rewarding? Absolutely.

Everyone Always Needs Somewhere to Live

Though the real estate market moves in cycles, one universal truth remains: everyone needs somewhere to live. People move for jobs, downsize due to retirement, or upgrade their homes to accommodate a growing family. Even when times are tough, a place to live is always a priority, no matter who you are or where you're located.

A Time-Tested Investment and Wealth-Building Strategy

Get-rich-quick schemes come and go. The stock market rises and falls. Real estate is forever. Property has been a wealth builder for generations, and that won't change any time soon. If you want to increase your wealth, investing in real estate is a great way to own a tangible asset that will stand the test of time.

Mostly Stable

Sure, the real estate market fluctuates. But overall, real estate is fairly predictable. If you hold on to a property long enough, its value will most likely appreciate. Rental properties generate consistent revenue. Tax benefits are available year after year. The train will keep moving, even if the journey includes peaks and valleys.

A Variety of Investment Options and Flexibility

Real estate investing is not one-size-fits-all. There are multiple options for investments, from residential to commercial and short-term to long-term. You can buy properties individually or through crowdsourced funding. You get to find the approach that works best for you, your family, and your wallet. When the time comes to change your approach, you also have the flexibility to make changes that suit you.

A Simple Business Model

The business model for real estate investing is pretty straightforward. Buy a property. Find a tenant. Collect payment. Use the cash flow to scale. You do not need to employ a complicated strategy to be successful. You simply start small, learn the business, execute, and scale. It's really that easy.

Buy Low and Negotiate

When you're buying a property, you have the power to negotiate. Your negotiation skills can help you acquire a property below the asking price or place the burden of some of the repairs on the seller. You also don't have to be a superstar negotiator to get started in real estate. It's a skill you can learn and use for life. As you hone your skills, you'll get even more bang for your buck as your business expands.

Many Ways to Profit

Collecting rent is not the only way to profit as a real estate investor. Tax benefits will put money in your pocket. Loan paydowns will, too, as will buying and holding properties to sell down the line. From vacation rentals to purchasing land for future development, real estate investing offers endless opportunities to turn a profit.

Pile Up Passive Income

Trust me, there is nothing better than making money while you sleep. Real estate investing is an incredible way to generate passive income, especially if you have the right systems and team in place to manage your properties. You can collect the cash while someone else deals with the details.

CONS OF REAL ESTATE INVESTING

Real estate investing can be a great way to generate income, grow your wealth, and take back your time, but it's not all fancy vacations and big checks. Like any business, it takes work to build a sustainable real estate company. It's important to know the truth about what you're getting into—cons included.

It Takes Time to Build Real Wealth

Real estate is a long game. It takes patience, persistence, and strategy to be successful. From making property improvements to finding quality tenants, it takes time to get things up and running. Once you do, though, the options are endless.

You Have to Be a Landlord and Manage Properties

Your properties are occupied by actual people, and people can be hard to predict. As a landlord, you'll have to deal with late payments and less-than-ideal tenants. You'll be responsible for handling maintenance and repairs. You will also have to ensure your properties are consistently filled so the money keeps coming in. Although you might be able to hand off these tasks to a property manager down the road, when you're first starting, these tasks will fall squarely on your shoulders.

You Have to Manage Paperwork and Bookkeeping

As a real estate investor, you won't just be touring properties, brokering deals, and doing DIY projects like you're on HGTV. Real estate requires a lot of paperwork, from contracts to logging expenses. Staying organized with your bookkeeping is essential. You won't be chained to your desk, but you will have to spend some time managing your business.

You Can Lose Your Money and Investment

Nothing is guaranteed in life. Real estate is no different. There's always a chance your investment won't produce the returns you anticipated. You can lose money, and it's important to understand that risk exists before diving into real estate.

TAKEAWAYS

Hyper-supply. Forced appreciation. Real estate cycles. The Big Four. We packed a lot into this chapter, but every piece of information is absolutely crucial to building your real estate knowledge.

At the end of each chapter in this book, I'll share a few key takeaways. These are things you'll want to remember as we move forward through the book.

Takeaway #1: The Real Estate Market Is Cyclical

After reading media coverage and talking with friends who recently made property purchases, you might be thinking you missed the boat to invest in real estate. You didn't. Every real estate market works through four cycles: recovery, expansion, hyper-supply, and recession. There are indicators to help you determine which phase of the cycle we're currently in and specific strategies to help you thrive during each phase.

Takeaway #2: Look at the Whole Picture When It Comes to Value

Savvy investors consider each element of the Big Four when it comes to real estate investing. Your property can generate value through natural and forced appreciation, cash flow, tax benefits, and loan paydowns. Use each of the Big Four components to your advantage to maximize the value of each investment.

Takeaway #3: Push Past Fear

The more you know about real estate investing, the braver you'll feel. When you understand the real estate cycle, you can adapt your strategy and hold strong when times seem tough. Understanding the Big Four will help you assess a property's potential in its entirety and make investment decisions confidently. And hopefully, knowing the pros and cons of real estate investment will help you dive in without hesitation.

Takeaway #4: Be Patient

Unless you're exceptionally lucky, plan on real estate investing to be a long game. As long as you do it right and know the risks, real estate investing can build significant generational wealth.

WHAT'S NEXT

You've got the basics of real estate down. Now it's time to lay the groundwork for purchasing your first property. In the next chapter, I'll help you pick a strategy, choose a property type and location, build your dream team, and prepare to finance your first deal.

2

EVERYTHING YOU NEED TO KNOW BEFORE BUYING YOUR FIRST PROPERTY

"Buy land, they're not making it anymore."

— *MARK TWAIN*

t this point, you're probably thinking something like this: *Alright, Andrew. I'm in. In fact, I'm texting my realtor buddy right now to set up some showings.*

Let me stop you right there. Put down the cell phone. Exit out of Zillow. Do not pass go. Do not collect $200. Just like Monopoly, you've got to learn the rules before you play the game. And if you want to dominate the game, you've got to have a plan.

In this chapter, we'll break down everything you need to think about before investing in your first property. From choosing a strategy to organizing the documents for your first loan, by the time you're finished with this chapter, you'll have a clear vision for your first purchase and be ready to hunt for your first deal.

CHOOSE A STRATEGY

Have you ever tried to lose weight? Before you started, you probably sought some advice from friends who have successfully dropped some pounds. Unsurprisingly, they probably had different suggestions for developing a diet and different preferences for exercising. They all achieved the same result by losing weight, but they all took different paths to get there.

Real estate investing is similar. If you talk to a dozen different investors, you'll find they each had different paths to success. All of the paths, though, can be traced back to one of the five options we're about to discuss.

So, how do you pick the right one for you? Start by asking yourself these three questions:

1. What are your goals? Consider whether you're seeing cash flow, quick returns, or a hands-off investment.
2. Are you willing to handle property management and repairs, or do you want to be more hands-off?
3. Can you handle the ups and downs of the real estate cycle in your local market and nationally?

Keep these answers in mind as you read through these strategies. We'll look at each of them individually.

Long-Term Rentals

A long-term real estate strategy is pretty simple if you have a little patience. When you use a long-term approach, you buy and hold onto properties for the future, possibly even for decades.

You might hold onto your investment for years, but that doesn't mean you have to wait to realize a return. The key to a long-term strategy is to use your rental properties to grow your overall portfolio. To do this, you need to be able to charge enough for rent to cover your mortgage and expenses with a little left over to pay down, build equity, and roll cash into additional properties.

Are long-term rentals right for you? Here's what you should consider:

- **They typically have lease terms of 12 months or more.** Thanks to these lengthy leases, you can anticipate a reliable income. Since this income is funding your mortgage, you can hold on to these properties for longer periods of time, leaving room for the value to appreciate over time.

- **They require less upfront capital.** You can typically find better terms from a lender for a long-term property. These units also aren't expected to be furnished and, due to lower turnover, require less maintenance between tenants.
- **Longer leases can lead to headaches.** A bad tenant might be difficult to remove from your property. There are fewer chances to increase rent, which means you might lose out on some income while you wait out a 12-month lease.
- **Consider the costs.** You might need to perform updates to make the property renter-friendly as well as maintain the property once people move in. If you're comfortable being a landlord, you can save money on property management fees. Long-term rentals have less turnover than short-term or vacation rentals, which means you might not need a full-time property manager if you're comfortable handling property maintenance tasks yourself as they pop up.

Short-Term Rentals

Finding (or creating) a great vacation rental can mean tons of extra cash in your pocket. These properties can often outearn long-term rental properties. The key is to have a place you can keep fully booked while accepting that you'll have to spend more time preparing the house between visitors.

Both of these options are appealing to real estate investors. Before you decide to pursue short-term rentals, though, here are a few things to think about:

- **There's a lot of earning potential.** Since these properties have tons of turnover, there are plenty of opportunities to raise rent prices to keep up with market changes.
- **You can stay hands-off.** You can hire a property manager, cleaning crew, and maintenance crew to keep your day-to-day involvement in the property at a minimum. Hiring a

team increases your expenses but makes this approach more passive, especially if you have enough properties and turnover to justify the cost.

- **Location is crucial.** You need to find the right property in the right vacation spot to see the returns needed to make your bank account soar.
- **They can be unpredictable.** You might end up with more vacancies than expected, especially during the offseason. And unlike with a long-term rental, you need to fill your unit with more customers more regularly instead of just finding one good tenant and watching the rent checks roll in for a year.
- **You need to provide some extras to renters.** These rentals need to be fully furnished. You are also on the hook for more costs than a long-term rental because you'll be responsible for listing fees on sites like Airbnb, utility costs, and extras like Wi-Fi.

Mid-Term Rentals

Mid-term rentals are typically booked for short terms, usually in increments of several months. These furnished properties are often located near a hospital, university, or corporate headquarters. Ideal renters include traveling nurses, students, and consultants who need consistent housing for several weeks or months but won't need a long-term lease.

Some real estate investors begin with short-term rentals and shift to mid-term because there tends to be less turnover and, thus, higher profits.

Mid-term rentals can be very appealing, especially if you are in the right location. Here's what to think about before pursuing this strategy:

- **There's demand for this type of rental.** Remote work is here to stay, which makes mid-term rentals very appealing. Since remote workers can work from anywhere, many travel to desirable locations and live and work there for several months at a time.

- **They're a short-term and long-term hybrid.** If you're undecided between a short-term and long-term strategy, a mid-term rental can offer the best of both worlds. They provide the stability of guaranteed rental income for several months at a time. You can also raise rent several times throughout the year since there is turnover every few months.
- **You won't be able to price these at the top of the market.** Typically, short-term rentals can fetch the highest rent, while long-term rentals garner slightly lower prices because tenants are locked in for a longer period of time. Mid-term rentals place you squarely in the middle of the marketplace.
- **You'll need more tenants.** Shorter lease terms mean more turnover. Platforms like Airbnb and VRBO can help you find renters, but be aware that this approach means you will have to prepare the property for new tenants several times per year.
- **Plan accordingly for additional costs.** You have to furnish the property after purchase since tenants won't be moving their furniture in for a short lease. Costs can also mount because you need to get the property move-in ready several times a year.

House Hacking

When you house hack, you rent out part of your home to other tenants. The rent you collect can go toward paying off your mortgage or additional expenses. House hacking is how I started in real estate, and it can be a great way to get your feet wet when it comes to rentals.

The key to house hacking is to have the right type of property. Duplexes and triplexes are popular house hacking options, as are homes with guest houses or garage apartments. Even purchasing land can be a house-hacking opportunity. A large piece of property can house several RVs or trailer homes.

Trust me when I tell you that house hacking has some serious benefits—and some drawbacks. Before you put a listing on Craigslist, consider the following aspects of house hacking:

- **It's favorable for financing.** Since these properties are considered owner-occupied, it might be easier to obtain financing.
- **It will free up a lot of cash.** If you are able to charge enough to cover your mortgage—and then some—you can roll more of your own money into additional properties. It's the start of your empire.
- **Your tenants will literally be your neighbors.** You will be in close proximity to your renters. If they're good tenants, this should be manageable. If they're not good tenants, it could make for a difficult living arrangement.
- **You'll have to be a hands-on landlord.** Your tenants will have more access to you due to your proximity to them. You also need to act as a legal landlord, which means you are subject to local and state laws.
- **You need to have the right property.** Your property needs to be suitable for renters, which might require some renovations. These preparations might include adding or updating a guest house or apartment, or making upgrades to the other side of a duplex.

BRRR (Buy, Rehab, Rent, Refinance, Repeat)

For this strategy, the process is literally in the name. You buy a property, make improvements, rent it out, complete a cash-out refinance, and then purchase your next property.

A cash-out refinance means you convert your equity into cash as your home loan matures. You gain equity as your home value increases or as you pay down your mortgage principal. Once you've built equity, you can refinance and borrow more than you owe on your house.

Confused? Let's look at a real-life example, step by step:

Step 1: You purchase a home for $250,000.

Step 2: You improve the home and rent it out. After 18 months, you've paid off $50,000.You still owe $200,000, so you decide to do a cash-out refinance.

Step 3: You refinance and add a portion of your equity to your new mortgage principal. In this case, you decide to add $30,000. When your new mortgage closes, you'll receive $30,000 that you can use to purchase your next property.

Ready to reno? Think about these things before you don your hard hat:

- **You need to find the right property at the right price.** In order to make this approach work, you'll need to find a distressed property to rejuvenate. You can often find these properties at a discount.
- **There's more effort involved.** You have to handle the rehabilitation, then bring in renters who will contribute to your cash flow. The good news is that their rent will help you pay down your mortgage quicker so you can move to the refinance phase.
- **Financing can be tricky.** Sometimes, purchasing and rehabbing a distressed property can be an uphill battle. It can be difficult to obtain a mortgage for a highly-distressed property.
- **You need a solid plan for renovations.** You also need to do substantial work to make the property livable and attract renters. You should feel confident you can complete these renovations properly on your own or can afford to hire help.
- **Costs can add up quickly.** Property owners often have to sink additional funds into the property to make the necessary—and likely substantial—renovations. The refinancing process also costs money because the property will need to be reappraised.

Which Strategy Is Right for You?

Now that you know the ins and outs of each strategy, it's time to compare them so you can pick the best option for you. We'll talk more about the numbers you need to know to evaluate a property in chapter 3. But until then, let's take a closer look at the difference between long-term, mid-term, and short-term strategies. For this exercise, we're going to pretend we are looking for a property in Nashville, Tennessee.

I picked Nashville because you could effectively run each strategy in the city. It is a popular spot for relocation, and many companies are moving their headquarters there. It is home to a university and several hospitals, so it could be a good fit for a mid-term strategy. It is also a popular tourist location with plenty of events, so it could be a good fit for a short-term strategy.

First, we will use Rentometer to check rent prices in the area. I used Vanderbilt University as the address since it is located downtown. The average rent within a half-mile radius is $2,794.

I'm also going to do my best to estimate my expenses. The median selling price for a home in Nashville is $433,000, according to Realtor.com. But let's assume that I find an incredible diamond in the rough for a little less than that and plan to pay $385,000 for a property with two bedrooms and one bath.

I now need to calculate my mortgage payment, which I can do using a mortgage calculator. For this example, I'm going to use Rocket Mortgage. Nashville is an expensive market, and I'm a new investor, so I'll have to put down less than 20% for a down payment. If I put down $35,000 and choose a 30-year loan term at 6.5% interest, my mortgage will be $2,212.24 just for principal and interest.

Rocket Mortgage also lets me calculate taxes and insurance using their calculator. My estimated taxes will be $112.29, and my estimated insurance will be $131.54. That brings my total estimated mortgage payment to $2,456.07. Over the course of the year, I can expect to pay $29,472.84.

I also need to determine how much I should save for capital expenditures, like maintenance, repairs, and upgrades to the property. There are different ways to calculate this expense. Generally, you should start by saving 1-2% of the purchase price each year for capital expenditures. For this example, that would be $3,850.

Long-Term Rentals by the Numbers

If I purchase a property in Nashville and sign a tenant to a 12-month lease, I can expect to make $33,528 in rental income. To find my expected overall profit, I have to subtract my estimated expenses for the property.

My estimated expenses for this property are:

- Monthly mortgage payments (including insurance and taxes): $2,456.07
- Annual capital expenditures: $3,850

When I subtract these expenses from my rental income, my annual profit is $205.16.

Mid-Term Rentals by the Numbers

Nashville is a healthcare hub. Let's look at the income I can make if I turn my property into a mid-term rental with three-month contracts to accommodate traveling nurses. I will have the chance to reevaluate my rental price every three months.

I decided to price my unit slightly over the average rent at $2,900 per month. With every new tenant, I can raise the rent. Let's assume I raise it by 3% with each new tenant. Here's what my rental income will look like by month:

January: $2,900
February: $2,900
March: $2,900
April: $2,987
May: $2,987
June $2,987
July: $3,076.61
August: $3,076.61
September: $3,076.61
October: $3,168.91

November: $3,168.91

December: $3,168.91

My total rental income for the year would be $36,397.56. Again, you'd have to consider your expenses to turn over the unit, taxes, repairs, as well as mortgage payments. I will have to turn over the apartment four times in this scenario.

Let's assume the turnover cost is $1,000 for each new tenant. That means my expenses will be:

- Monthly mortgage payments (including insurance and taxes): $2,456.07
- Annual capital expenditures: $3,850
- Annual turnover costs: $4,000

In this scenario, you would lose $925.28 after calculating your expenses. With that said, now's a great time to note that you will run into scenarios where you lose money with a strategy. That doesn't mean you should necessarily abandon that strategy. In this example, I could continue to play around with different down payment amounts, property prices, and lease terms to get a clear picture of my likelihood of success with a mid-term rental in the Nashville area.

Short-Term Rentals by the Numbers

Nashville is a popular tourist location, with visitors flocking from all over the country for bachelorette parties, music festivals, and sporting events. According to AirDNA, the average occupancy rate for a short-term rental is 41%, with a nightly rate of $262.10.

If I turn my property into a short-term rental, let's assume I will have renters for 15 days every month. My average monthly rental income would be $3,931.50 per month, which totals $47,178 per year.

I'll mention one last time that expenses will vary for a short-term rental compared to a long or mid-term property. There will be more turnover, which means more fees and possibly more maintenance costs. I'll also have to pay property taxes and my mortgage. I'll also need to cover monthly utilities, like electricity and WiFi.

Let's assume that between fees and utilities, I need to set aside an extra $400 per month. That brings my expenses to:

- Monthly mortgage payments (including insurance and taxes): $2,456.07
- Annual capital expenditures: $3,850
- Annual utilities: $4,800

After subtracting expenses, I will make $9,055.16. Of course, my expenses don't include a property manager or cleaning fees, the latter of which could fluctuate per month based on the length of the stay. I also didn't account for state or local taxes for these short, mid, or long-term strategies. My tax burden will depend on a variety of factors, including how my business is set up.

As you consider these strategies, run your own analysis based on your location and property prices. We'll look more closely at different property types and how to find the right investment location in the next few sections of this chapter.

CHOOSE A PROPERTY TYPE

Once you've picked an investment strategy to pursue, you'll have to choose what type of property you want to work with. Each property type has its own set of pros and cons. There's no right or wrong answer here. You'll need to weigh your options and pick the one that works best for you right now.

Residential Properties

Where do you sleep at night? Whether you're in a city apartment or a farmhouse in the country, if you call it home, it's likely a residential property.

A residential property is a home inhabited by the owner or tenants. In the rental world, this means you'll have tenants on a lease or rental agreement. These properties are specifically zoned for residential use.

We'll get into the specific aspects of each type of residential property soon. But before we do, let's review some overall pros and cons of residential properties.

One of the biggest advantages of residential rentals is income stability. Your tenants will likely be on lease agreements, so you can count on their income each month. You'll also have an advantage if you've purchased property before because you'll be familiar with the process.

However, it's important to know that residential properties have additional tax rules you'll need to follow. When you rent, you become a landlord, which means additional responsibilities and liabilities. You'll want to consider hiring a property manager or educating yourself on your duties as a landlord.

Let's take a closer look at each of your options for residential properties, including the pros and cons of each.

Single-Family Properties

A single-family home is just that: a home that is occupied by one family. From starter homes to mega-mansions, if it's designed to host a single-family unit, it falls in this category. These property types are appealing to renters because they offer privacy and space.

Single-family rentals can be desirable and lucrative because:

- **They often appreciate in value.** Whether you plan to sell quickly or hold on to the property long-term, they tend to go up in resale value.
- **They can be leased for longer periods of time.** People who rent single-family homes tend to sign longer-term leases. With a longer lease term, you can count on income stability and less tenant turnover.

For some people, single-family rentals aren't the right fit because:

- **They don't come with a lot of land.** Single-family homes often sit on smaller plots of land, especially in newer neighborhoods.
- **Desirable properties might not be in renter-friendly neighborhoods.** Some neighborhoods have limitations on rentals or high homeowners association fees that make renting unfeasible.

Multifamily Properties

A multifamily property can house more than one family at a time. In many cases, these properties are not owner-occupied and are rented out to tenants. Apartments, condominiums, mixed-use properties, retirement homes, and duplexes can all fall under this category. (Inspect, 2023)

Real estate investors choose multifamily properties because:

- **There's a tremendous potential for passive income.** Since you collect rent from multiple tenants, it often makes financial sense to hire a property manager. This makes the investment truly passive on your part.
- **There are substantial financial benefits.** Multifamily properties are eligible for financial advantages like tax benefits and are often well-positioned for discounts on insurance policies.
- **It's easier to weather vacancies.** If you have a 20-unit property and one unit is vacant, it's a manageable setback, not a disaster. If you don't have a renter for your single-family property, your income grinds to a halt.

Despite their perks, multifamily properties typically aren't popular choices for first-time investors. This is often because:

- **They require more of an investment.** Due to their size, these types of properties require a hefty down payment, which can be hard for new investors to pull together. You also need to hire a property manager if you want your investment to be truly passive.

- **There is a lot of competition.** These properties are desirable, so when they come on the market, competition tends to be fierce. Experienced investors will have enough cash on hand to make more desirable offers, making it hard for new investors to break in.

Townhome Properties

Townhomes are becoming increasingly popular, especially for people who want a neighborhood feel at a lower price point. Not convinced? In 2021, the construction of townhomes leaped by 28.1%, according to the National Association of Home Builders.

A townhouse typically shares a wall or two with neighboring properties but has its own entrance. Many also have their own backyards. Townhouses are also becoming more widespread and can be found everywhere, from densely populated cities to suburban communities.

Townhomes are an appealing investment option because:

- **Some renters prefer them.** Townhomes offer personal privacy, backyards, and fewer shared walls, making them more appealing to some renters than a condo or apartment.
- **They are a reliable mid-price rental option.** Townhome rental prices typically hover in the middle of the market. They also tend to recover their value after an economic downturn.

Townhomes still have some limitations. If you're considering investing in a townhome, keep in mind that:

- **They are susceptible to market downturns.** Yes, townhouses will eventually recover their value. But that tends to take time, which might be difficult for investors to stomach.
- **There isn't a lot of opportunity for forced appreciation.** Due to homeowners association guidelines, it's typically difficult to make external modifications to a townhome.

There are limits to internal upgrades as well. So, while you likely won't be able to adjust the floor plan, you should be able to make cosmetic changes to key areas like the kitchen or bathroom.

REOs/Foreclosures

Foreclosures are unfortunate, but they can also provide an opportunity for new investors. A foreclosure occurs when the homeowner does not make their mortgage payments and the house is repossessed by the lender. The lender then sells the house to recoup costs.

If a foreclosure is not sold at the right price to cover a loan, it becomes REO, or real estate owned. This means that it is owned by the lender and will often be sold at a deep discount.

A foreclosure can be a great opportunity for a deal because:

- **Lenders want to sell quickly.** The longer a lender holds on to a property, the more money they lose. This usually means you can find excellent deals. If you purchase an REO, you will also not have to worry about outstanding debts on the property.
- **You might not need a loan.** Since these properties are cheap, you might be able to purchase one outright.

Purchasing a foreclosure can be tempting, but there are several potential pitfalls. For instance:

- **What you see is what you get when you purchase an REO.** You'll be responsible for any renovations and major repairs. You can also expect to pay a bit more to get the property in rental shape since they are typically not maintained by the lender.
- **You might inherit something you didn't expect.** If you purchase a multifamily home in foreclosure, you might still have tenants to manage. And while an REO will not have any outstanding debts or liens, a foreclosure might.

You'll need to be very careful to ensure debts are cleared so you can take ownership.

Fixer-Uppers

These properties are typically purchased at a below-market price and have, to put it kindly, seen better days. Nonetheless, this type of property could end up being a gem in your real estate portfolio if you're willing to put in the work.

Some of the benefits of a fixer-upper include:

- **You can see a serious return on your investment.** Not only can you purchase the down-and-out property at a lower price, but your renovations could add substantial value to the property. This can help you earn a higher price when the time comes to sell.
- **You have options after the renovations.** Some investors will finish their property revamp and immediately put the house on the market to get a return on their investment. Others will hang on to the property and rent it while it appreciates in value.

A fixer-upper isn't all demos and decor, though. You'll also have to understand that:

- **You're not just getting a house—you're getting a project.** Renovations can be expensive, and you could run into unexpected issues that drive the price up even further.
- **You might have to wait to sell.** Depending on the stage you are at in the real estate cycle, the home—even with all of its upgrades—might sit on the market for a while. If your goal was a fast flip, this delay could lead to financial problems.

Mobile Home Parks

Due to its unique setup, a mobile home park might be your ticket to a thriving real estate business. A mobile home park is a large piece of land divided into smaller lots for mobile homes. The tenant owns a mobile home and rents the land from the property owner.

In addition to the individual lots, many mobile home parks offer the opportunity for multiple streams of income through laundry facilities, vending machines, and storage units.

Mobile home parks tend to be under-the-radar investment opportunities, but they can be real gems because:

- **They are relatively stable investments.** Since they are an affordable housing option, there tends to be consistent demand for them, regardless of the economic landscape. It's also hard to move a mobile home, so tenants tend to stay put.
- **You split responsibility with the tenant.** While you are responsible for the land in a mobile home park, the tenant is responsible for their home. This joint responsibility creates an incentive for both parties to work together to maintain and improve the park.

Mobile home parks can be lucrative, but they certainly aren't perfect. For example:

- **You have less control.** Since your tenants are responsible for their property, upkeep and maintenance fall on them. If they fail to maintain their property, it can impact your park's overall value.
- **There is less opportunity for appreciation.** Appreciation is usually created through upgrades by the owner.

Commercial Properties

From the office building you trek to every morning for your 9-to-5 job to the coffee shop you frequent for your favorite drink, you spend a lot of time in commercial properties. All of those properties are owned by someone—and that someone could be you down the road.

A commercial property generates profit through rental income or capital gain and typically functions as a business. Tenants are typically businesses that lease space on the property for longer lease periods compared to residential properties.

Commercial properties run the gamut from apartment homes to vacant land. Here's a breakdown of each one, along with benefits and drawbacks:

Apartments

Apartments and other multifamily rentals straddle the line between commercial and residential properties. Though they still serve as residences for people, they generate an income for whoever owns them.

Apartments can be a great commercial property investment because:

- **They provide diverse income streams.** Rent is a huge profit driver, but it doesn't stop there. On-site laundry facilities and parking packages can also generate additional income.
- **You can grow your portfolio quickly.** Since these properties create substantial cash flow, you can bankroll more properties to grow your business.

You'll still have your share of headaches, though. Some of the cons include:

- **More tenants, more problems.** Apartments need regular maintenance, and often, the requests for repairs never stop. Even with a property manager, there will be some oversight required on your part, as well as money to finance the repairs.
- **Delayed gratification.** This approach requires patience. Apartment complex purchases take time to close and, depending on your location and other market conditions, can take longer to sell if you determine they aren't the right fit for you.

Condos

Condos are both individually and collectively owned. In other words, people independently own the individual units but share ownership of the common areas. Typically, a homeowners association manages the common areas. The overall building or complex is usually owned by a builder or group.

Purchasing an individual condo can be a great purchase for new investors because:

- **They are fairly easy to manage.** You are responsible for what happens inside the walls of the condo unit, but everything outside of that falls on the homeowners association.
- **There are lower overall costs.** The price to purchase a condo is typically lower than a single-family home.

Still, a condo can come with its own set of challenges. You'll need to consider that:

- **They tend to appreciate slowly.** Don't expect immediate appreciation from a condo. They tend to climb in value more slowly than their counterparts.
- **You can expect additional fees.** Owners typically pay a monthly fee to the homeowners or condo association to maintain other parts of the property. These fees can be pricey, so plan accordingly.

Retail

A retail space houses businesses like shops and restaurants. These properties can feature one business, like a grocery store, or several, like an outdoor shopping center (Tross, 2023).

If you're thinking about investing in a retail property, keep in mind that:

- **You can charge higher rental prices.** If you have an excellent location, retailers will flock to your property. You can charge accordingly, and you'll earn even more if you can host multiple storefronts in one plaza.

- **The renter has substantial responsibility.** Though you're responsible for maintaining the property, the business owner is responsible for taking care of most of the interior upkeep.

You might experience some of these drawbacks:

- **A lot of capital is needed.** These properties are not cheap. Most commercial properties, retail included, require a substantial upfront investment.
- **There are a lot of leases to manage.** If you own a space with multiple tenants, you'll need to manage multiple leases that might start and end at different times. This will impact your cash flow, so you'll need to be on the ball to make sure you don't end up with multiple vacancies.

Office Space

From skyscrapers to office parks, office buildings—and investment opportunities—are everywhere. These properties are classified into three categories depending on their features.

Class A properties are the most prestigious, featuring upgrades that allow owners to charge above-average rental prices. Class B is the middle tier, with standard finishes and average rent prices. Class C properties are typically for groups that need function over fancy finishes.

These properties are worth considering because:

- **They have longer leases.** Rental agreements for office spaces tend to start at 5-7 years.
- **Your tenants will handle upgrades.** As with retail properties, tenants will often invest in aesthetic upgrades to suit their businesses. In most cases, they are also responsible for furnishing the office space.

Investing in office space also means wading into a rapidly changing real estate market. You should know that:

- **Vacancies can be costly.** In this space, you want to hang on to your tenants, which means building strong relationships. This requires checking in throughout the terms of the lease.
- **The market is changing post-COVID.** As more companies move to permanent remote work, office vacancies might become more prevalent. You need to have a deep understanding of the demand for office space in your market to make wise investment decisions.

Land

That piece of vacant land you drive past every day might just be the real estate investment you've been waiting for. When you have the right property, land can become a valuable asset you can use to rent or develop. The best part? Land tends to appreciate more quickly than other properties.

Renting

When you own a piece of land, you can rent it to others to use for farming or housing. These types of agreements can benefit both the tenant and the property owner.

Here's what to consider before tying yourself to a land investment:

- **The leases are very long.** Some commercial lease terms can be extremely long—we're talking 50 years or more. Therefore, you can count on a guaranteed steady income.
- **The costs are lower.** If you have a tenant, they will often handle improvements. If you rent your land for hunting or fishing, you'll also incur fewer costs.

Renting land isn't necessarily a straightforward process. Some of the potential drawbacks include:

- **You typically need the help of a professional.** Depending on whom you're leasing to and the terms of the agreement, you might need a lawyer to help with the paperwork.
- **There are laws and regulations to consider.** For example, if you plan to lease the land to a company that will be mining natural resources, you might run into red tape. You'll need to do due diligence to ensure the land can be used as you intend.

Developing

Developing a piece of land means you build a structure on a piece of vacant property. You could build on land yourself by adding a house or commercial space, or flip the land to a developer through an outright sale or a contract-to-purchase.

If you're ready to jump into land development, consider that:

- **A high-growth area is key.** Land is limited, so finding the right piece of property in an area that is experiencing a lot of growth can be very lucrative.
- **You will have multiple options for development.** If the property is large enough, you can subdivide it and flip it to multiple people. You could also sell the entire chunk of land to another developer.

Of course, not all land is zoned for development. That perfect piece of land might not be a good option for development if:

- **It's not zoned for the type of development you have in mind.** You have to determine if the land is zoned for commercial or residential development before making your purchase.

ASSEMBLE YOUR TEAM

Michael Jordan needed Scottie Pippen. Emmett Smith needed Michael Irvin and Troy Aikman. Greg Maddux needed Tom Glavine and John Smoltz.

In other words, every great victory starts with a great team. If you want to rack up wins in real estate, you need a strong team around you. Here's how to build one.

The Core Team

These are your ride-or-dies. They're the people you'll call on time and time again as you launch your business and guide its growth. Consider this group your starting five.

Your Spouse or Significant Other

My girlfriend (now my wife) was the guiding force behind my real estate journey. She knew the industry and helped answer my questions. Whether your spouse is interested in real estate or not, you'll need their support as you pour your time, energy, and money into new investments.

Mentor

This book is meant to be a blueprint for your business. However, your specific needs and circumstances are unique to you. That's where a mentor comes in. They'll supplement what you learn from this book. Find someone in real estate who is a few steps ahead of you and take them to coffee. Build a relationship with them and don't be afraid to ask them questions. You'll soon find they'll be an invaluable part of your growth.

Investor-Friendly Real Estate Agent

The real estate agent you used to purchase your home might not be the best option as you move into investing. An investor-friendly agent will have a deep knowledge of the real estate investing space and possibly be an investor themselves. They will also have a broad network in your desired market, which will help you access off-market properties and find the best tradesmen to help with renovations.

Lender

Your ideal lender shares many of the same qualifications as your ideal real estate agent. They should know the nuances of real estate investing and the specific types of loans you plan to pursue.

Ideally, they'll be able to help you navigate creative financing options, which we'll cover later in this book.

Insurance Agent

You'll need to insure your properties, and that's never cheap. As your portfolio grows, so will your insurance needs. An investor-friendly insurance agent can walk you through various coverage methods that will work for your portfolio, like master policies, layered policies, quote share policies, and loss-limited policies.

You'll also need different types of coverage for different types of properties, like tenant legal liability for a residential property.

Bench Players

There's a reason why the NBA has a Sixth Man of the Year Award. The people on your bench can sometimes be the difference between mediocrity and true excellence. Now that you've assembled your core team, it's time to build your bench. As your portfolio grows, you'll rely on this group more and more.

Contractors

When the plumbing breaks or the roof needs to be repaired, who are you going to call? Hopefully, a trusted contractor. The best time to start searching for a contractor is before you need them, so start compiling your list now. Ask for recommendations and keep their numbers handy so you can move quickly when you need assistance.

Bookkeeper

Rent's coming in, money's going out. Your books can become a massive mess if you aren't diligent. You can DIY this part of your business for a while, but as you grow, look for a bookkeeper with real estate experience to help you keep everything in order.

CPA

Your bookkeeper will handle day-to-day tracking. A certified public accountant (CPA) will handle the big-picture stuff, like your taxes. You won't need a CPA the day you open your business, but be prepared to make this hire once your business starts to grow.

Lawyer

When it comes to real estate, there's a lot more to think about besides just selecting a property. A real estate lawyer will help you navigate the buying and selling process and the leasing laws in your area, and draw up the necessary paperwork to protect your assets.

Property Manager

If you truly want your real estate business to generate passive income, you'll need a property manager to handle day-to-day operations like scheduling repairs and dealing with tenants. Ask for referrals and take your time with this hire since they will represent your business in tenant interactions.

Licensed Property Inspector

A licensed property inspector will physically examine the property from foundation to roof to identify a property's shortcomings and potentially expensive repairs. Whether the seller is willing to mitigate some issues or not, you'll want to know about problems with the foundation, roof, home's structure, water damage and mold, not-up-to-code electrical work, a leaky natural gas furnace, and so on.

ASSEMBLE YOUR PERSONAL FINANCES

We've spent most of this chapter talking about strategy, and you've probably had a lot of fun dreaming about your first property. Now, it's time for the not-so-fun part: going through your personal finances.

Step 1: Take Financial Inventory

Do you have cash saved, or are you in debt? Does your current job feel stable, or are layoffs looming?

Now's the time to pull up your bank statements, investment accounts, tax returns, and credit card statements to determine your financial health. Tally up your assets and liabilities. Your assets are things that have value, like your primary residence and cash savings. Your liabilities are things like your car loan or debt. You need a clear picture of your financial health before you invest in real estate properties.

Step 2: Set Realistic Goals and Expectations

If you have a poor credit score and little cash savings, you might not be able to start your real estate journey just yet. If you are in excellent financial standing with cash on hand, you might be able to acquire a property or two and get the ball rolling quickly.

After you've finished your financial inventory, set some realistic and attainable goals for yourself. Then, make a plan to reach them as soon as possible.

Step 3: Reduce debt and increase your credit score

If you're seeking an investment property loan, you'll need a credit score of at least 640 to qualify—and possibly 700 or higher if you plan on purchasing a multifamily property. You'll also want to start paying down your debt to give yourself more flexibility and limit your financial responsibilities (Ceizyk, 2023).

Step 4: Save for Your Initial Investment

You'll need money for a down payment, closing fees, and appraisal costs, among other things. Pick a target and start saving. Many landlords try to save at least 15% for a down payment on a rental property.

Once you know how much money you plan to save, look into your financing options. You might learn that your lender can only finance up to a certain amount, and you'll need more money to make up the gap. Plan ahead!

Step 5: Emergency Funds and Risk Management

A rental property is a risk. You could have several months or years when a property is unoccupied, or you might experience a downturn in your real estate market. Before you purchase a property, it is crucial to examine your emergency fund and assess if you have enough to cover the unexpected.

Hopefully, you already have an emergency fund for unexpected events like job loss or medical emergencies. You'll need a similar fund for your real estate ventures.

Here are some recommendations to jumpstart your planning:

- You should have an emergency fund for each property you purchase with enough money to go to cash flow expenses like HVAC repair or vacancies.
- If you plan to renovate an investment property, build an emergency fund of 10% for unexpected expenses.
- If you plan to manage rental properties, your emergency fund should total 15% of your annual combined rent.

Just like in Step 4, pick a savings target and put money aside each month to combat any unexpected emergencies. Trust me—you'll be glad you did.

PREPARE TO FINANCE YOUR DEAL

Someday, you'll have a team of people available to help you prepare for and finance your deals. Until then, you're going to have to do it yourself. I'm about to show you how.

Know Your Financing Options and How They Work

Unless you have a couple hundred thousand dollars just sitting around, you'll need financing to fund your real estate purchase. The first step is knowing your financing options.

Cash

If you have enough money to pay for your property in full, you'll be able to make a cash-only offer. This type of offer might give you an edge in a competitive market and provide you with immediate cash flow once you finalize the deal.

However, this locks you into one rental. If you have enough money on hand to make a cash-only offer, you have enough to finance multiple properties and supercharge your growth.

Your other option is cash offer financing. In this scenario, your financing company will make the offer on your desired property and pay for it in cash while you make payments to the financing company.

Conventional Loans

When most people talk about home financing, they are talking about conventional loans. These loans are mortgages, typically on a 15-year or 30-year term. You'll need a down payment and, if you put down less than 20%, private mortgage insurance (PMI) to obtain a conventional loan. Your lender will also consider your credit score and debt-to-income ratio to determine if you qualify.

Conventional loans are typically conforming loans, meaning they meet criteria from the Federal Housing Finance Agency.

Portfolio Loans

Portfolio loans are usually non-conforming conventional loans, meaning they don't meet Federal Housing Finance Agency criteria. When you have a portfolio loan, your lender keeps and services the loan in their own portfolio. These loans are not sold on the secondary market. These types of loans are often used by people who are self-employed or have a low credit score.

A portfolio loan can be an attractive option for borrowers because it can be obtained quickly and for a higher loan amount.

DOING A TRADITIONAL LOAN? HERE'S HOW TO GET APPROVED

To get a traditional loan, you'll need to get preapproved. You can apply for a traditional loan through a bank or lender online or by going to one in person. Applying online will be a quicker process, but going in person will help you build a relationship with your lender, which could be beneficial to you as your business grows.

Gather Your Documents

Grab your laptop and park yourself next to your filing cabinet. It's time to do some paperwork. Here's what you'll need to get preapproved:

- Tax returns from the last two years
- W2s from the last two years
- Pay stubs from the last two months
- Personal financial statements that outline your assets and liabilities
- Bank statements from the last two months
- Descriptions of other properties you own
- Purchase and sale documents for the property you want to purchase, if available

Know Where Your Down Payment and Closing Costs Are Coming From

Are you funding your purchase through your cash savings or a gift? Ideally, you'll have enough saved for your down payment and additional closing costs when you apply for your loan. When you are preapproved for a loan, the lender will put a limit on how long the preapproval will last. Most of the time, a preapproval will have a 90-day limit, so you'll want to seek preapproval when you are actually ready to buy.

What to Do If You Have No Money and Bad Credit

Real estate investing is not just for the rich. There are creative ways to finance your first property, even if you have no money and bad credit. We'll cover some of your options in chapter 4. Until then, develop a savings plan and a plan to improve your credit. Both will help you in the long run.

Partnerships and Investors

If you're eyeing more expensive properties, like a retail space or large multifamily property, it might be hard to come up with enough money to finance the deal. If that's the case, you could find an investor or partner to provide some additional capital.

Develop a business plan and start searching for your ideal partner. Your core team might be able to help you connect with potential investors. Meet them in person and vet them thoroughly before entering into a deal with them.

Takeaways

Whew! There's a lot to think about before making your first real estate purchase. From picking a strategy to seeking financing, there's a lot of preparation involved if you want to knock your first investment out of the park.

Here are a few key takeaways from this chapter to keep in mind as we move forward.

Takeaway #1: Don't Rush the Process

You want to have your ducks in a row strategically and financially before you start pursuing a property. I get it—it can be difficult to slow down when you feel like you were ready to start investing yesterday. Taking the time to develop a strong strategy and think through your purchase will help you in the grand scheme of things.

Takeaway #2: Do Your Homework

From picking a strategy to building a team to deciding on a financing option, it is vital to educate yourself. Great real estate investors are constantly learning and always do their due diligence before making a decision.

Takeaway #3: Pick a Path and Commit

If you decide you want to start your real estate journey by house hacking, focus on house hacking. If you decide you want to own mid-term rentals, focus on mid-term rentals. It can be so easy to pick one strategy, like house hacking and then get distracted by a great deal on a retail property. Remember, you can always pivot later. But for now, pick a strategy, pick a property, pick a location, and dial in. Focus is what will make you the big bucks.

What's Next

You've done the dirty work. Now it's time to have a little bit of fun. With your strategy outline, your team in place, and your preapproval letter in hand, you're ready to start hunting for an incredible deal. In the next chapter, we'll go over how to find and analyze your first deal.

FREE GIFT #1

The Must-Have Property Buying Checklist: you don't know what you don't know!

How do you know what kind of property to buy? Make your property purchases seamless with this essential checklist. Designed to help you cover the crucial steps and considerations, from evaluating the property's condition and market value to understanding financing options this checklist can help you avoid common pitfalls and make the best-informed decisions.

To access this free bonus, head to https://readstreetpress.com/rentalgift1 in your internet browser or scan the QR code below and I'll send it to you right away!

3

HOW TO FIND AMAZING DEALS
NO ONE ELSE CAN

"Every person who invests in well-selected real estate in a growing section of a prosperous community adopts the surest and safest method of becoming independent, for real estate is the basis of wealth."

— *THEODORE ROOSEVELT*

You're driving through a new neighborhood, and suddenly, it happens. Your eyes land on the duplex you thought only existed in your dreams. It needs a little TLC, but it's not in total disrepair. It's fifteen minutes from the nearest hospital and five minutes from a grocery store. And it's for sale. The clouds part. The sun lands on the duplex roof like a spotlight. You swear you hear the angels sing.

Then you wake up.

Chances are, you are not going to stumble upon your ideal investment property by accident. It's going to take some elbow grease, a bit of research, and a well-maintained network to find an amazing deal.

But it's not impossible. In this chapter, I'll show you everything you need to know to not only find an incredible deal, but analyze it so you can be sure you're not wasting your hard-earned money.

Let the hunt begin!

THE FOUR PHASES OF THE REAL ESTATE CYCLE

"This too shall pass."

You've heard this saying before, probably more times than you can count. And although it wasn't originally uttered about real estate, it's especially applicable to property investing.

The real estate market is cyclical. A good real estate investor—that will be you!—will understand the nuances of the real estate cycle, know how to identify the different phases, and adjust their strategies accordingly.

The length of a real estate cycle fluctuates, but on average, each one spans about 18 years.

This isn't guesswork, either. Homer Hoyt, who pioneered real estate market analysis and eventually became the chief economist of the Federal Housing Association, first identified the cycle in 1933 after studying land values in Chicago. The cycle is still widely used by investors today to guide their decision-making. The key word here is "average." Hoyt's cycle is a good guideline, but some cycles last much longer than 18 years. Others will be shorter.

In other words, don't pull out your calendar and start marking the arrival and departure of each phase of the cycle just yet. You won't be able to identify which phase we're currently in by looking at your calendar or even browsing Zillow. The real estate cycle is closely connected to other parts of the global and national economy. Global events can cause ripple effects in the real estate industry, which we saw firsthand during the COVID-19 pandemic. Outside factors like inflation, unemployment, and interest rates can impact the real estate cycle, as can shifting demographics. For example, a large business moving its headquarters to a new city could lead to a new phase of the real estate cycle in that housing market. An extreme event like COVID-19 can cause further turmoil.

Regardless of how long each real estate cycle lasts, they will still include four distinct phases: recovery, expansion, hyper-supply, and recession. Let's look at them one by one.

Recovery

In many cases, this phase begins while a region or even the whole country is still in the midst of a recession, and many people are still feeling the pain of tightening their purse strings. Different areas of the country may be experiencing downturns while others are thriving; this dynamic can change constantly. To the average eye, it looks like nothing is happening because new construction is at a standstill. Although it's a difficult time for many people in a region that's struggling economically, it can be an opportunity for investors.

How to identify the recovery phase: You'll start to notice declining vacancies in the market and see an uptick in people looking for new leases. You might also notice a few more foreclosures on the market.

Your strategy: In the recovery stage, vigilance is key. The signs of recovery are often subtle, so good real estate inventors need to be observant and act quickly when opportunities arise. This is the time to pursue below-market value properties and put in some elbow grease into making them rental gems. To make the most of this phase, you'll want to be in a financial position to act quickly on opportunities and wait out the rest of the recovery phase.

Expansion

You know that feeling you get during those first few glorious days of spring when the sun starts to shine a little brighter and the air feels a little warmer? That's the expansion phase of the real estate cycle. In this phase, people are becoming more confident in the economy. They're finding jobs and seeing a little more cash in their pocket. They feel better about making big purchases and might be ready to move.

During this phase, supply has not caught up to housing demand. Instead, there are fewer units available, which drives rent and housing prices up until new inventory comes on the market.

How to identify the expansion phase: You'll start to notice unemployment decreasing. You'll see construction companies break ground on new construction. You might also hear people grumbling about inflation or read a news story about rising interest rates.

Your strategy: Give the market what it wants. Now's the time to update existing properties or pursue new investments that align with people's tastes. With the right upgrades, you can often sell properties above market value to buyers looking for updated homes. In other words, now's the time to invest and upgrade.

The other part of the strategy—and the mark of a great real estate investor—is to stay calm. During this phase, people tend to panic-buy, especially as banks adjust lending requirements and people fear they're about to miss out on a real estate peak. Falling victim to panic leads to mistakes, so you'll need to be vigilant to avoid the panic trap.

Hyper-Supply

The expansion phase leads to heightened demand for housing. Businesses scurry to meet that demand, which leads to a frenzy of investors and developers rushing to increase the housing supply. Inevitably, the market reaches a tipping point, and housing supply begins to exceed demand. Sometimes, this is entirely due to too much inventory. In other instances, an outside factor like a sudden economic shift can lead to a pullback. When that happens, we've entered the hyper-supply phase.

How to identify the hyper-supply phase: You'll notice an uptick in vacancies even as construction continues at a high volume. You'll see properties remain on the market longer, often accompanied by rapid price reductions. Unemployment might rise, and the Federal Reserve might announce lowered interest rates.

Your strategy: It's easy to panic when the hyper-supply phase sets in. Panicked property owners tend to make poor decisions, like liquidating assets if they are vacant. Instead, it's best to hold strong. If you have some extra capital, buying and holding property can also be an effective strategy to survive the hyper-supply phase.

Recession

If you're in the real estate game long enough, you will experience a recession. It's a natural part of the real estate cycle. During a recession, housing supply far exceeds demand. Property owners often have their properties vacant, or they significantly decrease rental rates to accommodate the economic downturn.

How to identify the recession phase: Remember all that ongoing construction in the hyper-supply phase? That comes to an end. Since inventory now far exceeds demand, rental rates begin to drop as housing prices stabilize.

Your strategy: The best time to prepare for a recession is before it happens. You should have a rainy day fund for scenarios like this. Recessions can also be a prime opportunity to expand your portfolio if you can. Keep an eye out for foreclosures that you can purchase and hold on to until the recession passes.

CHOOSE A LOCATION

You've picked an investment strategy and property type. Now the real work begins.

In many cases, the success of your real estate business will come down to location. You could find the best deal on the best property for your chosen strategy, but if the property isn't in the right location, you'll struggle to see the return on your investment that you wanted. Keep in mind the phase that your intended geographical location is in. You may wish to consider a different location to invest in if yours currently doesn't present the ideal conditions.

That's why the best real estate investors spend a lot of time learning how to evaluate a property's location and conduct plenty of due diligence prior to making a purchase.

Local or Long-Distance

Do you want to be within driving distance of your properties, or are you willing to pursue properties in other towns or states to meet your goals? Buying locally is often a good start for first-time investors because you know the area and will be able to manage the property in person. You'll also save money since many lenders consider out-of-state properties to be higher risk.

Of course, this all depends on where you live. Some real estate markets are better than others, so you'll have to run the numbers to see if purchasing out-of-state is worth the effort. Include things like taxes and insurance rates in your calculations.

Neighborhood Demographics

When it comes to real estate, the neighborhood matters. Think carefully about who your ideal renters will be. A young, newly married couple might be willing to pay top dollar for a townhouse if it's in a desirable, walkable downtown neighborhood. A family with young children might be desperate to move into a suburban neighborhood with lush parks and a nearby school.

As you research a property, look at statistics for the neighborhood, like home values and median income levels. This data will help you determine if your purchase will net the rental price you desire.

Job and Unemployment Rates

Can your ideal renter afford to lease your property? Monitoring job and unemployment rates can help you find a property that is in a thriving area. The Bureau of Labor Statistics offers monthly job reports that will help you track changes in median annual wage and overall employment levels.

Population Growth

A growing city means more potential renters for your property, whether your property is a single-family home or a retail space. Population growth will help you understand what type of demand there might be for your property. Before you purchase a property, calculate the population growth of your area.

Let's say you wanted to calculate population growth for your city over the last three years. Start by determining how many people lived in the city three years ago and how many live there now. Subtract the initial population from the current population and divide it by the initial population. Then multiply that number by 100. You'll end up with a percentage for the population growth over the last three years. Divide that number by three to determine the average growth rate per year.

Proximity to Businesses and Amenities

No one likes a long commute. Consider how far your potential property is from local amenities and high-traffic business areas. For example, determine how far your investment will be from the nearest grocery store or the entrance ramp to the freeway. For instance, a mid-term rental near a hospital will be very desirable for traveling nurses. A home 30 minutes away will be less desirable.

School Districts

If you will be renting to families, the quality of the school district your property is zoned for is incredibly important. In 2023, 30% of buyers between the ages of 33 and 42 considered the school district to be the top factor for choosing their home, according to the National Association of Realtors Home Buyers and Sellers Generational Trend Report. In other words, a good school district allows you to charge premium rental prices.

Use resources like Great Schools or Public School Review to research the quality of the schools in your area. If you are purchasing property locally, check with your network to get their feedback on schools in your area, especially if they have children.

Price-to-Rent Ratio

The price-to-rent ratio compares home prices to annualized rent. To calculate it, divide the median home price by the median annual rent. This calculation will help you determine whether the property you are considering is overpriced or not. It will also tell you whether people are more likely to buy or rent.

Trulia offers some recommendations for evaluating the ratio:

Ratio of 1-15: Buying is more favorable
Ratio of 16-20: Renting is typically more favorable
Ratio of 21+: Renting is more favorable

Property Tax and Insurance Rates

Property tax and insurance rates fluctuate based on where your property is located. To calculate property tax, multiply your property's assessed value by the local tax rate. You might also want to seek quotes for insurance. A property in a neighborhood that is prone to vandalism or weather events might mean you'll pay a higher insurance premium.

Vacancy Rates

A city's vacancy rate tells you how many units are currently occupied. If you are purchasing a multifamily property, you will want to determine the vacancy rate for that particular property. You might also want to determine the vacancy rate for neighboring properties and the city where the property is located.

A real estate agency or other landlords can help you determine the vacancy rate for your area. You can also check the U.S. Census.

FIND THE DEAL

Real estate investors don't stumble onto great deals. They seek them out—or, in some cases, create them. You can have the same results, even if you don't have years of real estate experience.

Here's the biggest secret I can give you if you want to find a superb deal: know what you're looking for and know where to look.

Here's how.

Create Your Buy Box

You need to know what you're looking for before you even think about searching for a property. To do this, you need to create your buy box. Your buy box is essentially a list of criteria for your property.

Let's walk through an example together. I want my next property to be a long-term multifamily rental in Wisconsin. Here's a peek at my buy box.

Location	Green Bay, Wisconsin
Property Type	Duplex
Price Range	$200,000 - $250,000
Investment Strategy	Long-term rental
Property Size	Two units

I'll use this buy box to evaluate every property I encounter. A property should meet all this criteria to be considered a serious investment option.

Call Your Investor-Friendly Real Estate Agent

In chapter 2, we covered why it's crucial to have a real estate agent with investing experience. They will understand why you have the criteria you have for your purchase and adhere to your criteria when they present you with properties. Your agent will also have the latest information on houses about to come on the market and be able to offer guidance that will help you find the best deal.

Search for Off-Market Deals

Your ideal property might never make it online. Approximately 11% of home transactions are completed without ever listing the property, according to the 2021 Home Buyer and Seller Generational Trends Report from the National Association of Realtors.

An off-market property is not listed in the Multiple Listing Service (MLS) database. These properties are often off-market because sellers want to list the property privately or it is in foreclosure with tenants. Your realtor and your own network are your best bets for hearing about off-market listings in time to make a bid.

· · ·

Launch a Direct Mail Campaign

Launching a direct mail campaign is cheap and easy, making it a popular approach for new investors looking for their first real estate deal.

A direct mail campaign is pretty simple: you send letters or postcards directly to homeowners that outline your interest in buying their property. You can target specific neighborhoods or types of properties for your first campaign. Generate printed mailers or write a handwritten note targeting your potential seller's pain points, drop it in the mailbox, and wait.

Check Eviction and Foreclosure Records

You'll have to do some digging to find this information, but it might result in the perfect investment property. You can use a website like foreclosure.com to search for pre-foreclosure properties in your area. When you find one that meets your criteria, you can reach out to the property owner and negotiate a deal.

Reach Out to Wholesalers

A real estate wholesaler is essentially a middleman between a buyer and a seller. They purchase a property from the seller and find a buyer to purchase the home at a higher price.

For example, let's pretend a wholesaler in your area finds a distressed property and purchases it from the owner for a discounted price of $150,000. He sells it to an investor for $165,000 and pockets the difference while the buyer fixes up the property.

Drive for Dollars

The last way to find great real estate deals involves some good, old-fashioned shoe leather. Or, in this day and age, fuel for your car.

This approach is pretty self-explanatory. Using the criteria in your buy box, you pick neighborhoods or areas to explore, hop in your car, and drive around looking for deals. You might find a property for sale or locate the address of a vacant property so you can send a letter directly to the owner.

ANALYZE THE DEAL

After weeks of searching, you've finally found it: the property that will help make you rich. It's a great duplex that hits every single criterion in your buy box.

It's perfect. But is it a good deal? A property can look like an excellent investment when you're standing in its front yard. It can look like a disaster once you pull out your calculator and start running some numbers.

It is absolutely critical to analyze every aspect of the property and potential deal before moving forward with a purchase. I cannot stress this enough. You might feel pressure to snap up a property immediately. Don't give in to this impulse. Instead, walk through the process I am about to show you to fully analyze the deal.

Research the Location and Comparables from Other Properties

In chapter 2, we went over some of the factors to consider when you are analyzing a potential real estate market. Now that you have a specific property in mind, we're going to review those factors again. Remember, this analysis includes things like school districts, proximity to businesses and amenities, and specific fees like taxes and homeowners association fees.

In addition, you'll want to consider the neighborhood. Is it growing? Are there plans for expansion or additional amenities?

Furthermore, you'll want to research comparables (or "comps") from other properties. To do this, you need to find several on-the-market or recently sold properties that are similar to the property you are considering.

You'll refine your process for searching for comps over time, but here's the typical workflow:

- **List your home's specifications:** A comp does not have to be a direct replica of your property, but it should be similar to the property in terms of location, condition, property style, property age, square footage, number of bedrooms and bathrooms, and renovations.

- **Conduct an online search for similar properties:** Use the search feature on a site like Zillow or have your real estate agent search the local MLS for similar properties. Do not limit your search to properties that are still on the market. You should look at properties sold within the last six months.
- **Identify your comps:** You might find a bunch of properties that fit your criteria or just a few. Keep your list to four to six properties and make sure they are as close to your potential property as possible.
- **Hit the road:** Drive past the properties to get a feel for their curb appeal and identify anything an online listing might not show, like excessive road noise or nearby construction.
- **Calculate your property's market value:** Use these comps to identify your potential property's market value. You can average the sales price of the homes. You can also calculate the average price per square foot of your comps, multiply that number by the square footage of your property, and use that calculation to understand your property's market value.

Know and Run the Numbers

After you've looked at comps and researched your property's location, it's time to run some numbers.

For this section, we're going to imagine we've found the perfect long-term rental in an up-and-coming Green Bay neighborhood. It's a four-bedroom, two-bath home near breweries, shops, and hiking trails. It's the perfect rental for a young family new to the area and wanting to explore before purchasing a home, or for a group of young professionals willing to live with roommates.

This home is priced at $165,000. You can put down $20,000, and your mortgage will be $972 per month without property taxes and insurance. With the property taxes and insurance, you are paying

$1,306 per month. Now that you're armed with this info, it's time to pull out your calculator.

How to Analyze a Deal and What Questions to Ask

The calculations we are about to make require some additional information and numbers. You need to ask yourself things like:

How much can I charge each month for rent?

Look at rental prices in the surrounding area and for similar properties to estimate this number. For our sample property, we'll be able to charge at the higher end of the market because there aren't many houses of that size available. We expect to earn $2,500 per month.

How much will it cost to maintain the property?

In other words, what are your operating costs? These costs can include things like property management fees, repairs, and maintenance. They also include marketing and advertising to generate interest in the property. They do not include your mortgage payment or capital expenditures. Many investors estimate that operating expenses will total half of the annual rental income.

In this case, we are going to manage the property ourselves. We plan to advertise the property in a few Facebook groups, so costs will be low. Let's assume that for this property, our annual operating expenses are 50% of the rental income annually, so around $15,000.

How much will it cost to make the property rentable?

If you need to do a major renovation or upgrade, consider those costs as you analyze your deal.

Numbers to Know

These numbers are not difficult to calculate, but they are vital to understanding whether you are truly getting a good deal.

Here are nine numbers you need to know before purchasing a property:

. . .

Net Operating Income (NOI)

NOI = Gross operating income - operating expenses

When you know your net operating income, you can better assess how much money a property will generate, which helps you determine the overall value. This number is also needed to make some of the other calculations in this section.

How to Calculate NOI

Your gross operating income is all of the income you expect your property to generate over the course of the year, including rent, parking fees, and fees from any amenities you might have on the property. In our example, we are just collecting rent from tenants. Your operating expenses are what were outlined in the previous section: property taxes, maintenance, advertising, and so on.

See NOI in Action

In our example, we are just collecting rent from tenants. Here are the numbers:

- Annual operating income: $30,000
- Annual operating expenses: $15,000
- $30,000 - $15,000 = $15,000 NOI

Cash Flow Before Taxes (CFBT)

CFBT = NOI - Debt Service - Capital Expenses + Loan Additions

Before you make a purchase, you need to make sure you will receive the desired return on your investment. This calculation takes your debt into account.

How to Calculate CFBT

We've already calculated your NOI. Your debt service is the amount you will pay on your mortgage over the course of the year. Your capital expenses are potential expenditures like a new air conditioner or other improvements. Loan additions are any money from a non-mortgage loan, like one you take out to improve the property. A loan addition can also be interest from the property, if applicable.

See CFBT in Action

To establish our CFBT, we need to use our NOI and debt service numbers. Here are the numbers:

- NOI: $15,000
- Monthly debt service (just principal and interest): $972/month
- Annual debt service: $11,664
- Capital expenditures: $1,000
- Interest on property: None
- $15,000 - $11,664 - $1,000 + 0 = $2,336 CFBT

Cash Flow After Taxes (CFAT)

CFAT = Cash flow before taxes - income tax

You need to pay taxes on your income, and rental property is no different. Income tax varies by state, so you'll need to know how your state operates in order to calculate this number.

How to Calculate (CFAT)

Research the income tax rate in your state or talk with an accountant. Take into account your tax bracket and other factors your state incorporates. Then, determine how much income tax you will pay on the rental income you will make from the property.

See CFAT in Action

Our example property is in Wisconsin, which has a state income tax rate ranging from 3.5% to 7.65%. Most people in Wisconsin pay 5.3%.

Here are the numbers:

- CFBT: $2,336
- Income tax: $795
- $2,336 - $795 = $1,541

Return on Investment (ROI)

ROI = (Ending value - starting value)/(Starting value)

You don't want to lose money on your purchase. ROI is a percentage that helps determine if your investment generates profit efficiently.

How to Calculate ROI

To calculate ROI, you have to establish two values: the starting value and the ending value. The starting value is your initial costs, like your down payment, closing costs, and any out-of-pocket expenses. The ending value is your annual income from the property, which you determine by subtracting your mortgage payment from your rental income.

See ROI in Action

We have to start by calculating our starting value and ending value. Here are the numbers:

- Down payment: $20,000
- Closing costs: $2,500
- Out-of-pocket expenses: $3,000
- $20,000 + $2,500 + $3,000 = $25,500

Our starting value is $25,500.

Now, we need to calculate the ending value. Here's the breakdown:

- Monthly rent: $2,500
- Monthly mortgage payment, including taxes: $1,306
- Monthly return: $1,194
- Annual return: $14,328

To calculate the ROI, we need to subtract the starting value from the ending value and divide it by the starting value. That brings our ROI to 42%.

Annualized ROI

Annualized ROI = ROI/years held

You probably won't hold on to this property forever. By calculating annualized ROI, you can determine how much to expect on average each year.

How to Calculate Annualized ROI

If you plan to sell the property, it's helpful to know the annualized ROI you can expect. To get this number, divide the ROI you just calculated by the number of years you plan to hold the property. Try this formula a few times with different values for the number of years held.

See Annualized ROI in Action

Let's assume we plan to hang on to this property for five years before selling it. Here's how we'd calculate the annualized ROI:

- ROI: 42%
- Years held: 5
- Annualized ROI: 8%

Capitalization Rate (cap rate = NOI/value)

Capitalization rate is an effective way to compare the potential return for different properties. It helps you assess the risk of purchasing a property. Keep in mind, though, that capitalization rate uses the total value of your property. If you aren't going to pay for the property in cash, it might not be the best comparison tool.

How to Calculate Capitalization Rate

To determine the capitalization rate of a property, divide NOI by the purchase price of the property.

See Capitalization Rate in Action

Even though we're going to use a mortgage to finance our imaginary property purchase, it's still worthwhile to calculate the capitalization rate. Here's the breakdown:

- NOI: $15,000
- Value: $165,000
- Capitalization Rate: 9%

Cash-on-Cash Return (CoC)

CoC = Annual cash flow/cash invested

Cash-on-cash return is a ratio that measures how your cash flow compares to the amount you've invested in a property.

How to Calculate CoC

For this calculation, you need to divide your annual cash flow by the amount you've invested. The amount you've invested includes your down payment, closing costs, and additional fees. Your annual cash flow, as always, is your revenue minus expenses.

See CoC in Action

This number is fairly simple to calculate, especially since we've already established both values.

Here's how it works:

- Annual cash flow: $15,000
- Value: $25,500
- CoC: 58%

Average Annual Return (ARR)

ARR = (ROI1+ROI2+ROI3)/years held

Your average annual return will require a little bit of guesswork. Earlier in this section, we determined our ROI for one year. If we plan to hold this property for five years, the ROI will change annually. If we can increase the rent and lower our expenses, we might have a higher ROI. If we face a downturn in the real estate market and have some costly repairs pop up on the property, we might see a lower ROI.

How to Calculate ARR

To calculate your ARR, estimate how much your ROI will change over the time period you own the property. Try to do a couple of versions of this calculation with varying ROI values and years held.

See ARR in Action

Let's assume our ROI increases by one percentage point every year for five years. Here's how we'd calculate ARR:

- ROI for year 1: 42%
- ROI for year 2: 43%
- ROI for year 3: 44%
- ROI for year 4: 45%
- ROI for year 5: 46%
- Years held: 5
- ARR: 44%

Internal Rate of Return (IRR)

IRR = (future value/present value)^(1/Number of Time Periods) - 1

The internal rate of return is just that: internal. It's a way to estimate how much your property will earn while you own it.

How to Calculate IRR

Most investors do not calculate IRR manually. You can use the IRR function in Excel or a similar program to calculate it.

What to Consider When Analyzing a Short-Term, Mid-Term, or Vacation Rental

We just walked through the numbers for a long-term rental. If you are planning to invest in a short-term, mid-term, or vacation rental, you will need to consider some additional costs.

- Since you aren't locking tenants into a long lease, you'll need to consider seasonality and demand for your property. Will you be able to keep it occupied all year, or will your income severely dip during the off-season?
- You'll also need to invest in more marketing or advertising or use a service like Airbnb to bring renters in. This adds an additional cost, like listing fees.

- Your expenses will be higher because you will have to turn over the unit more often and pay for utilities.

These factors shouldn't deter you from investing in a short-term, mid-term, or vacation rental. You'll just need to add these numbers to your calculations so you can accurately assess the property you are considering to ensure it is actually a good deal.

Paying in Cash vs. Getting a Loan

Some investors swear by paying in cash for properties. Others prefer to use other people's money and build their empires through bank loans. The route you choose will impact your analysis of the property.

Getting a loan is often the route of choice for first-time and seasoned investors alike. It requires less capital to make your first purchase and allows you to grow quickly. As your first property generates cash flow, you can roll that extra money into down payments for additional properties, allowing you to build your portfolio rapidly.

When you use a loan to purchase a property, you have to be ready for the potential downsides. If you choose the wrong property—or worse, properties—you could see its value depreciate sharply. And if you're depending on rental income to cover mortgages, any sustained vacancies can wreak havoc on your finances.

Some investors choose to pay in cash for real estate, which can be a useful strategy if you have enough cash on hand. Paying in cash means you won't have a mortgage, so all that extra rental income can go right into your pocket or be invested elsewhere.

Purchasing a property with cash also means you can move quickly when investment opportunities arise since you won't have to work with a lender to secure a loan. In extremely competitive markets, this type of speed is very helpful.

However, this approach will decrease your tax benefits and limit your buying power. Since you aren't using leverage to acquire more properties, your real estate venture will take longer to grow.

Compare Findings to Your Buy Box

Remember the buy box you created at the beginning of this chapter? It's time to revisit it. By now, you should have several properties you are considering for your investment and a list of all the numbers, like NOI, for each property.

Based on your calculations, which properties meet the criteria in your buy box and provide a return you are comfortable with? Remember, the goal is to build a sustainable real estate empire. You don't want to feel financially crushed by your first investment.

Consider Cash Flow and Appreciation

As you assess your potential investment, it's crucial to consider cash flow and appreciation. There are several ways to determine whether a property will provide good cash flow or not. Many real estate investors aim to have a cash flow that totals 10% of the purchase price each year. If cash flow is higher than that, even better!

You also want to estimate the appreciation. Can you make upgrades over time that lead to forced appreciation? Are there market indicators that lead you to believe the property will experience natural appreciation? Also, consider how long you plan to hold onto the property.

Rule of Thumb and Other Useful Formulas

Experienced investors tend to have some general principles or rules of thumb they follow to analyze a deal. I will give you a quick overview of some now to put you ahead of the game. Use what feels right to you and the property you're considering:

- **The 1% Rule:** With this rule, you aim to have the monthly rent on your property exceed 1% of the purchase price. Investors use this rule of thumb for lower-priced rental properties.
- **Debt Coverage Ratio (DCR):** This ratio is calculated by dividing a property's estimated NOI by the annual debt. You want to aim for a DCR of 1.3 or higher because that

means you'll have enough money to cover your mortgage payments each month and still generate cash flow.

- **Loan-to-Value (LTV):** An LTV compares the amount of your mortgage to the appraised value of the property. A high LTV can be risky, so many investors try to build equity in their properties quickly.

Why You Need to Visit a Property Before You Buy

Have you ever sold a house? If you have, this process will seem familiar. Before the photographer arrives, you go on a cleaning frenzy, making sure every speck of dust is swept and every counter crumb is wiped. You pull down all your photos from the wall and pack up your favorite tchotchkes and knickknacks. After all, you want the potential buyers to picture themselves in your house, not you.

You might also do a few surface-level repairs, patch some holes in the wall, and deep-clean the carpets. You break a sweat mowing your lawn, planting a few extra flowers, and giving your mailbox an extra coat of paint.

When the listing is posted, the photos look great. But they don't mention that creaky floorboard on the stairs or the railroad tracks just down the road, or show the neighbor's completely unkempt lawn.

In other words, a picture might be worth a thousand words, but driving to the property and looking at it for yourself is worth a million.

It is vital that you get in your car and physically see the property you are considering purchasing. Look at the condition of the interior and exterior of the home for yourself. Drive through the neighborhood at different times of the day to get a feel for the noise and traffic levels. While you're at it, swing by your comparable properties and be honest about your potential investment comps. Is your property in a better neighborhood? Is it on a noisy street? Does it look like the side gutters are hanging on for dear life?

Your eyes will tell you things that an online listing cannot. Look at properties for yourself and be honest about their actual value. Just because a property is cheap doesn't mean it's a good investment.

How to Identify Common Red Flags

Over time, you will learn how to spot red flags in property listings and on-site more easily. As you learn more about property repair and maintenance, you'll be able to spot costly repairs and shoddy workmanship instantly.

Until then, I'm here to help you spot some common red flags. Here's what I tend to look for:

- **Slow sellers:** This largely depends on your real estate market. If homes in your area are selling within a week and this one has been on the market for six months, be cautious. Ask yourself (and your realtor) why it's taken so long for the property to sell.
- **Quick flips:** If a home was purchased and put back on the market within a few months, it was likely flipped. Some investors are excellent at flipping houses and do solid work. Others take shortcuts, so you'll want to be wary and ask plenty of questions about the renovations done.
- **Water damage:** Water damage often leaves wet spots or yellow spots on walls and ceilings. Keep your eyes peeled for this type of damage when you tour a home. Mold mitigation, whether the seller is responsible for it or you are (in an as-is property—see below), may be necessary to protect the health of your tenants, preserve your property value, and even prevent lawsuits.
- **As-is listings:** If you purchase an as-is listing, you are responsible for every repair that pops up—and they could be major. Sellers are not obligated to tell you about some issues with an as-is property.
- **Roof condition:** You'll be able to see the condition of the roof from the road. Does it look old and neglected? Are shingles missing? Roofs are expensive, so you'll want to know what you're getting yourself into if you purchase that property.

Takeaways

Your first real estate investment is a big deal, and it can be really intimidating to make your first purchase. I had my share of sleepless nights when I purchased my first property, wondering if I was making the right call or setting myself up for a financial loss. I don't want you to feel that way, which is why I'm sharing my best tips in this book.

Here are a few key takeaways from this chapter before we talk more about financing:

Takeaway #1: Have a Vision

Your buy box is your vision for your investment. It is a crucial first step on your investing journey, so don't skip it. Have a clear idea of what you are looking for. It will help you eliminate bad fits quickly so you can spend more time on worthwhile properties.

Takeaway #2: Be Objective

Before you invest in a property, run the numbers. Use the formulas from earlier in this chapter to determine if the property is a good investment. Make a vow to yourself that these numbers—not your desires—will dictate your purchase. It can be so easy to fall in love with the property, realize the numbers don't work, and try everything in your power to manipulate the math so you can purchase it. Numbers do not lie. Use data, not dreams, to make your decision.

Takeaway #3: Do the Legwork

Literally—get in your car and drive around looking for gems. Walk the neighborhoods you love. Get on your hands and knees during a real estate tour and inspect the home. You will not find great deals from your couch. Get out in the world and hunt. This is the best part!

WHAT'S NEXT

You've created your buy box. You've found the property. You've analyzed the deal backward and forward. The answer is clear: this is it. This is the one. This is the property that will jumpstart your real estate portfolio and help you build the life you've always wanted.

It's time to make a deal. In the next chapter, we'll go over how to craft and close a real estate deal. Those house keys will be yours in no time!

4

HOW TO BUY ANY DEAL YOU WANT WITH TOTAL CONFIDENCE EVEN IF YOU HAVE NO MONEY AND BAD CREDIT

"I would give a thousand furlongs of sea for an acre of barren ground."

— *SHAKESPEARE*

You can picture it now. You have that first rental check in your hand. It's going to cover your mortgage and then some. Your first rental property is fully booked, and the money is finally coming in. In a few months, you'll have enough money to buy your second property, then your third, then your fourth.

It's a beautiful vision, isn't it? There's just one small problem.

Minor, really.

Miniscule, when you think about it.

You have no money. And you also have pretty bad credit, thanks to a few years when you were a little too swipe-happy with your credit card.

Alright, so maybe the problem is not so miniscule.

But all is not lost. There are plenty of ways to purchase property without an astronomical credit score and a huge down payment.

In this chapter, I'll show you your financing options, including a few creative ways to get financing without having your finances in tip-top shape. After that, we'll go over every single aspect of closing your first real estate deal, from submitting and negotiating an offer to doing due diligence to closing the deal.

You're going to hear the jingle-jangle of your new house keys in no time.

FINANCING OPTIONS

Many people dream of investing in real estate. Few take the plunge. Often, that's due to finances. They think they don't have enough money for a down payment or the capacity to take on a loan. Or, they think their poor credit score will prevent them from getting any type of loan.

That's not the case. There are plenty of financing options for new investors and people who are trying to obtain their second or third property. These financing options fall into two categories: traditional and creative. Let's look at both of them right now.

Traditional Financing

You do not need a 20% down payment to buy a home. In fact, you can obtain a conventional loan with just a 3% down payment.

But before we jump into the requirements for a traditional loan, let's go over the basics. A traditional or conventional loan is not backed by the government, but most of them conform to guidelines set by Fannie Mae and Freddie Mac.

These types of loans are the ones your parents and grandparents used to purchase their homes. The requirements usually include:

- A minimum credit score of 620
- A down payment of at least 3%
- A debt-to-income ratio below 43%
- Good credit history
- Proof of employment and income

If you meet these requirements, you should be able to obtain a conventional loan.

Creative Financing

If you have a bad credit score and little savings, you won't qualify for a traditional loan. Instead, you'll have to get creative. There are some unique ways to purchase property without obtaining a mortgage or a traditional loan. We're going to talk about five of them now.

Seller Financing

When you purchase a property through seller financing, you pay the seller of the property instead of the bank. The agreement is usually similar to a mortgage, but it eliminates the bank or lender. If your mortgage is issued to you from the seller, it is a purchase-money mortgage. These types of deals generally do not require a down payment or, in some cases, a credit check.

These types of agreements come in many forms, including:

- **Assumable mortgages:** This type of financing lets the buyer take over the seller's existing mortgage, which can sometimes carry lower interest rates.
- **Holding mortgages:** In this agreement, the seller provides the loan and holds onto the property title until the buyer pays for the property.

Seller financing can be a great option for people who want more flexible terms and lower closing costs. It's important, though, to use a professional to help negotiate this type of agreement since there are fewer protections for buyers.

Lease Options and Rent-to-Own Agreements

A rent-to-own agreement is a type of seller financing. This type of agreement lets the renter pay the seller an option fee that allows them to purchase the seller's property later.

A rent-to-own agreement includes a standard lease and an additional portion that specifies the option to buy. In many cases, a portion of the buyer's rent can be applied to the down payment or to the eventual purchase of the home.

You will also pay a nonrefundable option fee even if you decide not to move forward with the purchase.

A lease option is a type of rent-to-own agreement—and it's the preferable one for buyers. Lease options do not require you to purchase the home at the end of the lease, giving you the option to move on to other opportunities if the home isn't the right fit. If you pursue a rent-to-own agreement, take care to ensure that you have a lease-option contract so you can exit if needed.

These types of agreements are excellent options for people who just need more time to get their ducks in a row before purchasing a home. If you live in a high-priced market and would have trouble scraping together enough cash for a down payment, a rent-to-own agreement can help you with your first investment purchase.

Lease Purchase Agreements

Lease purchase and lease option agreements have a lot in common, but they differ in one critical aspect. In a lease purchase, you and the seller are locked into the sale unless something unforeseen happens.

The terms of the agreement are negotiated before a lease is signed. Often, the buyer will pay an above-market rate for rent so that the extra money can be put toward a down payment. Your agreement might also require you to pay insurance, property taxes, or maintenance costs.

The good news is that you can enter into these agreements without a high credit score, and you are contributing to the down payment every time you pay rent. It eliminates the feeling that you are throwing money away while renting because you are building equity.

However, you have to be in the financial position to buy the home at the end of the lease agreement. If you can't qualify for the mortgage, you might lose the ability to purchase the property.

HELOCs and Cash-Out Financing

A home equity line of credit (HELOC) allows you to borrow against the equity in your home. Then, you can use the house as collateral. It typically has a lower interest rate than other loans and is sometimes used to access an additional credit line for other purchases.

We talked about cash-out financing earlier in the book, but here's a refresher. A cash-out refinance enables you to take out a new loan that is worth more than what you currently owe on the house. When you close the deal, you get the difference between your new mortgage and the balance you owned on the previous loan in cash.

A HELOC is essentially a second mortgage since it is separate from your original mortgage. A cash-out refinance covers and eliminates your existing first mortgage. You still have a payment, but it replaces what you owe on your original mortgage.

The interest rates also vary. With a cash-out refinance, you can have a fixed rate or an adjustable rate, while a HELOC offers a variable interest rate.

These can be good options for investors who have already made a home purchase, but wouldn't be able to qualify or can't afford a new down payment. If you already have a property with equity, you can capitalize on that equity to expand your portfolio.

Owner Carrybacks

An owner carryback, also known as owner financing, is an option for people who cannot qualify for a mortgage. When you use an owner carryback mortgage, the loan is provided by the owner and carried by the owner.

When you enter into an agreement like this, the seller hangs on to the title of the property until the loan is fully paid off. In exchange, you make a down payment and take over paying their mortgage. The sale is completed through a deed transfer. At the end of the agreement, the buyer makes a balloon payment for the rest of the mortgage.

This approach is great for people who have poor credit or are strapped for cash. It's also used to seal deals quickly. It can be tricky to find sellers willing to enter into these types of agreements, though. The short loan terms and end-of-term balloon payment can be a burden for many buyers. You might also encounter a higher interest rate.

Why Creative Financing Can Be So Powerful

If you know and understand how to creatively finance a property purchase, you are well-positioned to thrive as a real estate investor.

For your first purchase, you might pursue creative financing out of necessity because of your financial situation. Having access to creative financing is a great thing because it means you don't have to be rich or have made perfect financial decisions in the past to pursue property ownership. Using one of the creative financing options I just described can help you enter the real estate market, and you just need one property to get the ball rolling.

If you don't need to use creative financing to purchase your first investment property, meaning you have a strong credit score and enough money for a substantial down payment, it's still important to understand your creative financing options. As your portfolio grows, you might run into scenarios where creative financing makes sense. For many investors, creative financing is a great alternative to traditional loans during a recession or in times of hyperinflation.

The Risks and Challenges of Creative Financing

Did you ever have to share an art project or writing piece in front of your classmates at school? It can be nerve-wracking to put your work out there. That feeling occurs because doing something creative comes with risks. Heck, writing this book is a risk for me!

Creative financing might not involve personally putting yourself out there, but it does require you to take on some element of risk. These types of financing agreements typically result in higher interest rates and more complicated terms than the traditional mortgage. In many cases, you're dealing directly with the seller, which can be a challenge.

Before you enter into a creative financing agreement, be sure you understand the agreement and are comfortable with the risks. For example, if you are entering using a HELOC, you will have an adjustable-rate mortgage, which means your interest payments could increase substantially. You risk being on the hook for higher payments in the future, so be sure you are comfortable with that.

SUBMIT YOUR OFFER

After you've picked your financing approach, it's time to submit your offer. Before you start drafting your offer, though, make sure you have two things in place: mortgage preapproval, if applicable, and a real estate agent.

Having mortgage preapproval will help make your offer appear more legitimate to the seller because you will have to complete several steps before approval. If you plan to use a traditional mortgage to purchase your property, get preapproved before you submit an offer, and, ideally, before you even start looking for a property.

You should also have a realtor you trust, preferably with experience in rental properties, in your corner before you submit an offer. This real estate agent will help you through the entire purchasing process, which should save you money in the long time. Trust me, if you're purchasing a property for the first time, a good realtor is worth their weight in gold. Pay the commission— it'll pay off down the road.

With all of that out of the way, let's walk through the offer process.

How to Make an Offer

Making an offer on a property is a multi-step process.

First, you'll need to do some research to settle on the price for your offer. This research should include looking at your comps and considering the competition from other buyers. The condition of the house and the time spent on the market might also weigh into your decision-making.

Second, you'll want to consider contingencies. A contingency is a clause that allows you to exit the deal with your earnest money. Contingency clauses are often tied to the home inspection. If you need financing, you might also ask for an appraisal or a financing contingency.

Third, you'll need to look at your budget. How much can you offer in earnest money? What monthly mortgage payment can you afford, and how does it compare to the rent you'll seek from tenants? Decide now what your limits are, and don't go over budget. If this deal doesn't work out, it's OK. There will be other properties. Don't blow your budget out of fear.

Fourth, you'll need to draft your offer letter, preferably with the help of your real estate agent. An offer letter is a detailed document that lays out your proposed terms and conditions for the sale.

What to Include in Your Offer

A real estate transaction is not a back-of-the-napkin deal. These types of transactions take time, and your offer letter is often just the start of negotiations with the seller. Whether you draft your offer letter or seek help from an experienced real estate agent, here's what you'll need to include:

Property Details

As with any important document, you need to outline the stakeholders involved. Include the name and address of yourself and the seller. You should also include the address of the property you want to purchase as well as any other important property specifications, like boundary lines or lot numbers.

Purchasing Information

Now's the time to propose your purchase price. Typically, your offer will be less than the price for which the property is listed. This is OK. Use your comps and your research to decide on a price you think is fair and make the offer. The seller will have a chance to respond.

If you are using financing, you can also include details about how you will pay for the property. You can include your preapproval letter or stipulate that you'll pay in cash.

You'll also want to outline how much you'll put down as an earnest money deposit. We'll talk about that more soon, but basically, it is a deposit that tells the buyer you are making a serious offer.

Contingencies

Your research on the property is not over when you submit your offer letter. You'll need to include details about how much time you'd like to complete your due diligence on the property and the ownership. This process might include inspections and official property searches to ensure you are dealing with the actual owner of the property.

You also need to include a contingency clause. You are not free and clear once your offer is accepted. You could discover a massive issue with the foundation during the inspection or run into an issue with your financing. Lay these contingencies out very clearly and specify that if they occur, you can exit the agreement without penalty.

Closing Dates

The buying process does not—and should not—go on forever. So, include your target date for the closing.

What Is an Earnest Money Deposit?

It can be hard to part with money before a deal is closed, but it's an important part of the buying process. An earnest money deposit is provided in good faith to show the seller you are serious about your offer and intend to buy the home.

If you want to receive your earnest money deposit back if the deal falls through, include that in your offer letter. You can ask to receive your earnest money back if the deal falls through due to something outlined in the contingency clause, or if the seller backs out for other reasons. You can also ask that the earnest money be applied to closing costs or the down payment.

Typically, buyers put down a deposit that totals 1%-3% of the price of the home. Earnest money can also be used as a negotiating tool in a competitive market. If the home is competitive, earnest money deposits can climb up to 10% of the purchase price.

After your offer is accepted, the earnest money is placed in an escrow account with a third party (Chase, 2021).

How to Get Your Offer Accepted

Creativity isn't limited to financing. You can be creative with your offer, too. The best real estate investors have some tricks up their sleeve to make their offers more enticing to sellers. The options are endless, and over time, you'll find a few go-tos. Here are a few of my favorites:

- **Appeal to the seller's motivations:** Your real estate agent might be able to help with this. People sell their homes for a variety of different reasons, and figuring out why your ideal property is on the market can help you beef up your offer. For example, if you learn that the seller is moving soon, you might be able to offer a quicker closing date to help them out.
- **Increase your earnest money deposit:** If you can, offer more earnest money. This gesture indicates just how serious you are about purchasing the house and can make the seller feel confident that the deal will actually close.
- **Increase your down payment:** The less financing you need, the more confident a seller can be that the deal will close. You can put down a large down payment to ensure the deal goes through or make an all-cash offer if you're able.
- **Offer financial incentives:** From offering to pay moving expenses to paying title insurance fees, you can sweeten your offer with some financial incentives.
- **Be thoughtful about contingencies:** The fewer contingencies in your offer, the better. In a highly

competitive market, waiving inspection or financing contingencies can help move your offer to the top of the pile. Just be sure you understand the risks of waiving contingencies.

You don't need to use all of these approaches in your offer. In fact, you should pick and choose which ones to use and when to use them. Consider how competitive your market is and the condition of the home before sweetening your offer. You might find you can close your deal without spending more money.

HOW TO NEGOTIATE

Negotiating a real estate deal is not like you've seen in the movies. There's no yelling or screaming, no staredowns, and often, no fancy boardroom with leather chairs and a long mahogany table.

Instead, most of your negotiating will be done through your agents and include a lot of text messages, number crunching, and paper documents. The process starts as soon as you submit your first offer.

How the Negotiation Process Works

You've finalized your offer and sent it over to the seller. Now, you wait.

When a seller receives your offer, they have three options: accept it, reject it outright, or counter.

If they accept it, congratulations! You're on your way to buying your first rental property and will need to finalize your financing and schedule your home inspection to keep the momentum going.

If they reject it outright, all is not lost. Sellers usually reject an offer because it is too low. If you're still set on purchasing the property, you can work with your agent to craft a new offer. If you don't think you'll be able to reach an agreement that's within your budget, though, move on and hunt for a different property.

If the seller counters, you'll have the chance to review the offer with the realtor and determine if it's worth accepting. If you're not happy with the counter, you can respond with another counteroffer. As you go through this process, you can use some of the strategies outlined in the previous section to sweeten your offer, like waiving contingencies or compromising on the closing date.

Tips for Success

In a perfect world, your first offer will be accepted for 100% of your real estate investment purchases. Unfortunately, we don't live in a perfect world. At some point in your real estate career, you'll have to negotiate.

When that time comes, whether it's on your first purchase or your fourth, I want you to win. These tips will help you do just that.

Play Out Different Scenarios Before Submitting Your Offer

A championship-caliber coach or athlete would never take the field without a solid game plan. You shouldn't submit an offer without one, either.

Before you submit your first offer, game plan how you'll respond in different scenarios. If you plan to offer $100,000 for a home the seller has priced at $150,000, what will you do if they counter at $140,000? Will you walk away? Counter at $110,000? Offer more earnest money?

Walk through every possible outcome and decide how you will react. Know your boundaries, too. Determine the highest price you can afford to pay for the property and stick with it. The last thing you want is buyer's remorse.

Arm Yourself with Data

When possible, back up your offer with data. If your offer is in line with comparable properties on the market, share that in your offer letter and during the negotiation process. Do your research and know your numbers.

If you'll have to put work into the house to make it livable, mention that as well. If the kitchen is out of date or needs new appliances, let the seller know that you've factored that cost into your offer.

Don't Let Your Emotions Take Over

Staying calm is key to winning a negotiation. Think before you respond to a counteroffer. Consider your personal boundaries in terms of price and contingencies.

Our emotions tend to take over when we feel unprepared. Keeping your emotions in check is easier if you've already gamed out different scenarios and done extensive research. Remember, if your offer is rejected or countered, it's not personal. Take a deep breath, put yourself in the seller's shoes, and work your plan.

How to Negotiate through Agents

Your real estate agent is your secret weapon when it comes to negotiating. You want your agent to be a creative problem solver with the backbone to hold firm to your requests when necessary.

A good agent will also be honest with you about what is possible during the negotiation process. They will let you know if your bid is way too low, and they will share ideas for creative incentives to add to your counter.

When you negotiate through an agent, the agent will review counteroffers with you and work with you to determine how you should respond. They'll offer advice and expertise based on their knowledge of the market and your goals. When you decide on a counter, they will negotiate with the listing agent, who will relay your offer to the seller. The process continues until the deal falls through or you reach an agreement and the deal closes.

Negotiation Skills and Creative Financing

You've heard the saying that practice makes perfect, and that's true for real estate negotiation. Your first negotiation won't be your best, but over time, you'll develop the skills you need to make yourself a negotiating powerhouse.

To become a better negotiator, practice:

- **Not taking things personally:** It's just business. Practice separating the seller from the offer. They are trying to act in their own best interests, just like you. Attack the problem instead of holding a grudge.

- **Asking questions:** Ask your realtor questions about the market, the property, and the seller. Be curious. Use what you learn to improve your offers and add incentives that appeal to the seller.
- **Walking away:** It's hard to do, but sometimes necessary. Know your limit and walk away from the process if you don't think you can reach an agreement with the seller.

You can also apply some of the creative financing approaches discussed earlier to your negotiation. For example, if the closing date is a sticking point for the seller, offer to let them lease back the property after closing until they move. Let your real estate agent know if you're open to creative financing approaches and use their expertise to enhance your negotiation.

DUE DILIGENCE

When you make an offer, you've usually only seen the house at a basic level. You know the layout and the general condition of the property. Even if you have a background in construction or a keen eye for home repairs, you still need to dig deep to find out if any potential issues are lurking beneath the surface of the home.

The time between when you reach an agreement with the seller and closing on the property is crucial. This is when you do your due diligence on every aspect of the property, from the finances to the overall condition.

Why Due Diligence Is Important

After you enter into an agreement with the seller, it is your responsibility to thoroughly research the property and ensure the property is acceptable. This process is called due diligence.

Due diligence is important because it lets you know if you're actually getting a good deal on the property. You don't want to purchase a property only to find out later that the house has massive flood damage or needs a new roof within the next year.

Effective due diligence examines the property from every angle, typically through careful inspection. As the buyer, you are responsible for hiring inspectors, so it's important to find people that you trust. Your real estate agent, mentor, or colleagues can provide recommendations for trustworthy and skilled inspectors.

Title Inspection

When you take over the title of a home, you don't want any surprises, like liens due to unpaid taxes or outstanding loans. Homes can also become embroiled in legal disputes, like divorces or disagreements over ownership.

A title company will help you discover these issues before your purchase is finalized. They'll verify the property information provided by the seller and conduct a thorough search for unpaid taxes, dues, easements, and other potential financial issues.

The company will also survey the property to determine the boundary lines and usually manages the closing process, including managing the earnest money in escrow.

Document Inspection

Review each and every document provided to you by the seller and your real estate agent. Ask questions about things you do not understand.

Some of these documents will include property disclosures, which can be found on the listing pages. Property disclosures can include things like appliance issues or any work the current owner plans to do before your closing date.

Physical Inspection

You aren't required to complete a physical home inspection—in fact, in highly competitive markets, sometimes people waive inspections altogether—but I highly recommend them. It is worth spending the money before the house closes to avoid a massive, expensive surprise later.

A basic home inspection covers the basic parts of the house and determines its condition. You should always work with a licensed inspector. During their inspection, they'll examine the entire structure as well as the electrical systems, appliances, waterlines, and more. They'll also provide a full report when the inspection is complete.

If you encounter surprises during the inspection, talk with your realtor about how to proceed. You might need to pull out of your deal, particularly if you encounter a problem outlined in the contingency clause.

Other Optional Inspections

A basic physical inspection won't catch every potential issue with a property. Some buyers choose to perform additional inspections, like radon inspections. In some cases, the home's age will impact the inspections you choose to have conducted on the property.

For older homes, you might want to consider having an asbestos inspection or a lead-based paint inspection. We now know that asbestos and lead can be very harmful to our health. So, you might find it is worth it to have an older home inspected for both issues.

CLOSE THE DEAL

Your new property passed the due diligence process with flying colors. Now, it's time to prepare for your closing date, which is when you'll officially get the keys to your new investment property.

Here's your to-do list as your closing date approaches.

Order Insurance

After your inspections are complete, it's time to start shopping for home insurance. Many lenders want to see proof of insurance in order to finalize your loan, so don't put off this step. You want to be able to shop around to find the best deal for your new property.

Before you shop for insurance, consult your lender to determine their requirements. Some will require you to prepay for a year of insurance and purchase a policy that covers rebuilding your home.

Depending on your location, you might also need flood or earthquake insurance.

Start shopping early. Most lenders want to see proof of insurance three business days before closing, and some want to see it even earlier. The more time you have to shop around, the better deal you'll find.

Set Up Your Business Entity

If you haven't already, set up your business entity before your closing. Most investors set up an LLC, S-corp, or a C-corp. Each option has its pros and cons, and all have different tax implications.

What Is an LLC?

A limited liability company (LLC) separates your real estate venture from you as an individual. You can buy, sell, and rent property through your LLC, and it protects you from personal liability for what occurs on the property.

The Pros and Cons of an LLC

An LLC reduces your personal liability for what happens on your property, like an injury. You can also add other people to the LLC, allowing you to build a business with investment partners.

While an LLC reduces your personal liability, it doesn't eliminate it completely. For example, you can still be held responsible for failing in your responsibilities as a landlord.

Tax Implications of an LLC

An LLC offers pass-through taxation, which means you pay personal income taxes. (Snyder, 2022) You can also transfer titles without being taxed on appreciating value, and qualify for additional deductions beyond what you receive when you file your personal tax return.

What Is an S-Corp?

An S-corporation, or S-corp, allows owners to shift their corporate income and associated finances to shareholders.

S-corps are appealing to inventors because they allow you to reduce your self-employment tax. This is because you only have to pay taxes on wages.

Like an LLC, a S-corp is a pass-through entity. However, it operates like a C-corp in that it must have bylaws, minutes for meetings, and a board of directors.

The Pros and Cons of an S-Corp

Reducing your self-employment tax can make an S-corp very appealing to real estate investors, but it isn't always the best option. If you plan to flip the property or be a property manager, saving on self-employment taxes can be a huge benefit. If you aren't going to be as hands-on with your property, an S-corp might hurt more than it helps.

It can be very difficult to remove property from an S-corp without tax implications. You also can't gift property from an S-corp, which can impact your future financial planning.

Tax Implications

If you aren't a passive real estate investor, you might be subject to self-employment tax. For example, if you purchase a property and flip it for profit quickly, that is not a passive investment and thus is subject to self-employment tax. If you have an S-corp, you can place your profit from the sale under the S-corp and pay yourself a portion of it as your wages. Your self-employment tax will be on your wages, not the entirety of the sale (Kaplan, 2024).

What Is a C-Corp?

A C-corporation, or C-corp, means the owners are taxed separately from the rest of the entity. They are essentially double-taxed because their profits are taxed at the corporate and personal level.

The biggest difference between an S-corp and a C-corp, besides taxation, is the amount of shareholders each entity can have. An S-corp cannot have more than 100 shareholders, while a C-corp can have an unlimited amount.

The Pros and Cons of a C-Corp

A C-corp offers liability protection since it is a separate entity from personal property. It's a great option for people who need to offer gains and incentives for capital investors. However, it limits your personal deductions and can be very difficult to maintain since there are a lot of requirements surrounding them.

Tax Implications

When you operate out of a C-corp, you open yourself up to more taxes. You will be taxed twice: at the corporate level and at the individual level. You'll also pay more in capital gains taxes if you sell the property and be subject to taxation if you transfer property out of the C-corp.

Final Walk-Through

Sing it with me—"it's the final countdown." The final walk-through is the last hurdle to clear before you can sign the paper-work and officially take ownership of your new property.

It is important to be thorough in the final walk-through because it is your last chance to check for issues and confirm that the house is in the expected condition.

As you participate in more walk-throughs, you'll learn more about what to look for. Until then, consider this your walk-through checklist:

- Use your inspection summary to check the condition of the house. Ensure every requested repair has been completed to code, if applicable.
- Ask for warranties or receipts for work on the home.
- Make sure the previous owner is completely moved out.
- Test every lock on every door and window.
- Check window screens for holes or tears.
- Run appliances to make sure they are functional.
- Check cabinets, refrigerator, and sinks for mold.
- Test every single outlet in every single room.
- Check for garbage and pests.
- Walk around the yard and perimeter of the property.

Your walk-through will likely happen several days before your closing date and last about an hour, depending on the size of the property. If you find an issue, you can ask the seller to fix it to delay the closing date.

Sign the Documents

Today's the day. Your closing date is the day you officially sign the paperwork for your new property, complete the sale, and receive the keys.

Your closing day will involve multiple people, including the sellers, real estate agents, lenders, title company representatives, and an attorney. You'll spend several hours signing paperwork to complete the sale. The documents might include a loan estimate, closing disclosure, mortgage note, initial escrow statement, mortgage, certificate of occupancy, and a purchase agreement. All of these documents. You will also pay closing costs and other escrow items, typically through a cashier's check or wire transfer.

TAKEAWAYS

If you have poor credit and no money, home ownership is not out of reach—you'll just need to get a little creative. In this chapter, we covered the entire home-buying process, from finding creative financing solutions to officially receiving the keys to your new investment.

Here are a few key takeaways from this chapter:

Takeaway #1: Think Positively

Traditional financing is not your only option when it comes to purchasing a property. Consider the creative options I've outlined in this chapter and pursue the one that works for you. Purchasing a home is a complicated process, no matter which financing option you choose. There will be times of frustration and delay. Be positive. Take a deep breath. It will all work out.

Takeaway #2: Have a Strategy

You need a strategy for financing your home. You also need a strategy when the time comes to make an offer. Always game-plan for different scenarios. Know your target price for the property and the highest amount you can afford before you submit your offer.

Takeaway #3: Don't Take Shortcuts

When it comes to purchasing property, you need to do your due diligence. Take your time on the title, document, and physical inspection process. Be thorough during the final walk-through. And when your closing date finally comes, read every document carefully

5

HOW TO CREATE AN EASY PROPERTY MANAGEMENT SYSTEM & AVOID ALL THE HEADACHES

"As a real estate professional, if you're trying to build a big business, you need to invest in that business."

— *GLENN SANFORD*

You've invested your time in researching an investment strategy. You've invested your money in your dream property. Now, it's time to invest in your processes.

As a real estate investor, your ability to effectively manage your properties will make or break your business. After all, to be a successful real estate mogul, you need to have multiple properties. And in order to have multiple properties that actually turn a profit, you need to be able to manage them.

To do this, you need to invest in your processes and your team. You need to be able to find good tenants and streamline the turnover process. You need a network of efficient and economical contractors you can trust.

In this chapter, I'm going to tell you exactly how to build the processes and team you need to keep your business running smoothly.

WHAT DOES A LANDLORD DO?

If you own a property and lease it out to tenants for payment, you are a landlord. Being a landlord means you are responsible for filling your property with tenants, appropriately maintaining the property, and following city, state, and federal regulations.

You can make big decisions about your property, like raising rent based on your agreement with tenants or evicting tenants if they fail to pay. You also have to make sure the property is in the proper condition for rentals and prepare it for new tenants.

It's a big job. But if you want that sweet passive income, you'll need to do a bit of heavy lifting.

Should You Hire a Property Manager?

If you or your business entity owns a property that is rented to others, you are a landlord. But you can outsource the day-to-day operations of maintaining the property to a property manager.

A property manager you can count on is worth their weight in gold. They can take plenty of time-consuming tasks off of your plate, like:

- **Coordinating maintenance:** A good property manager will have a list of reliable contractors who can help with maintenance and repairs.
- **Finding new tenants:** When you have a vacancy, a property manager can take the lead on finding a new tenant and researching the market value for a new lease agreement.
- **Vetting tenants:** A property manager can handle the background and credit check process to help you find the best possible tenant.
- **Collecting payment:** Your property manager can follow up with tenants if they miss a rental payment and help with the eviction process if needed.

In other words, you get to sit back and collect your rental checks while someone else does all the work. Sounds great, right?

Hold that thought. Property managers are like any other type of employee. Some are really good at their jobs; others aren't. Good ones aren't cheap, and for new investors, it's sometimes easier to handle these tasks yourself until you can afford an excellent property manager.

A property manager typically charges a percentage of the rental price. The cost can range from 6% to 12%, depending on your location and the property manager's experience. Their pay will reduce the cash flow for your rental, so you'll need to analyze your options carefully before making a hire.

Having a property manager also reduces the amount of control you have over your property. You're still the landlord, of course, but different property managers (or their companies) have different processes for screening tenants and handling repairs. They might also take a different approach to filling a vacancy than you would. If you're OK with having less control over the day-to-day operations of your rental, this won't be a problem.

Some real estate investors choose to manage their properties on their own. This is an excellent way to learn the nitty-gritty details of property and tenant management. If you decide to manage your first property on your own, don't be afraid to change course if the process becomes overwhelming. If you feel stressed about dealing with tenants and chasing down rent payments, consider outsourcing property management. Your peace of mind will offset the hit to your cash flow.

How to Prepare Your Property for Long-Term Tenants

Whether you hire a property manager or handle it yourself, the real work begins when it's time to prepare for tenants.

When you purchased your property, you had a target rental price in mind. Now, it's time to finalize your asking price and lease terms and draft the lease. You'll want to have the lease on hand and ready to go when you find the perfect tenant.

You will also need to review the legal requirements for rental properties in your area. Every city and state has different requirements. Make sure you know the rules and regulations before you list your property.

You'll also need to put in a bit of elbow grease—or hire someone else to put their elbow grease into the property instead. Start by inspecting the house from top to bottom for safety hazards and possible upgrades. You can handle the repairs yourself or hire a professional to make sure every repair is done correctly.

You'll also need to clean the property thoroughly to make it move-in ready. For most landlords, this process includes deep-cleaning the entire home, from the baseboards to the ceiling fans. You might also want to spruce up the property with a new coat of paint or updated flooring.

Long-term properties are not usually furnished. They do come with appliances, though, so you'll want to make sure every appliance is in proper working order. If an appliance seems to be on its last legs, start preparing to replace it.

Once your property is in tip-top rental condition and you have a property management plan in place, it's time to find your first tenant.

FINDING TENANTS

Ask your fellow landlords for their best tenant stories, and you're sure to hear some doozies. One will tell you about the tenant who left the home in shambles after an eviction. Another will tell you about the mystery stains they found throughout the house after tenants moved out, or the weird smell that took weeks to dissipate.

Your tenants are people. People come with issues. Eventually, you'll have a tenant you'd rather forget. If you screen tenants properly, though, great tenants will far outweigh the bad.

Here's how to find tenants who pay on time and treat your property as if it's their own.

How to List the Unit

When you list the unit, your goal is not only to find a good tenant but also to fetch the highest possible rental rate for the property. Your ability to do this hinges on your ability to market your property and all its features effectively.

How Much to Charge for Rent

When you purchased your property, you had an estimated monthly rental price in your head based on comparable properties in your area. This estimate is a great place to start as you nail down your official asking price. Remember that market values change over time, so conduct this analysis again before you officially list the property and anytime you bring in a new tenant.

You want your rental rate to be in line with the rest of the market. You also want it to align with the actual value of your property. When you purchased your property, you received an appraisal value for the home. If you made substantial improvements to the property, seek a reappraisal to determine the home's current value.

Many real estate investors aim to charge a monthly rent that is between 0.8% and 1.1% of the appraised value. For example, a home appraised at $300,000 might fetch between $2,400 and $3,300 in rent each month.

At the very least, you want to charge enough in rent to cover your monthly mortgage payment and, preferably, the rest of your expenses, like maintenance, insurance, and repairs.

Before you settle on a monthly rate, review the laws for your state and city. Some states, like California and New York, have rent control laws that will limit how much you can increase rates. Consult an attorney to make sure you understand the laws and restrictions.

How to Take Listing Photos

When you stand in line at the grocery store checkout, your eyes probably wander to the candy and magazines that separate the registers. What catches your eye? If you're anything like me, you're probably drawn to magazines with a striking headline or an eye-catching photo. Even if I don't care about the subject matter, the right cover is often enough to capture my attention while I wait to ring up my groceries. And if the cover is really good, I might even pick up the magazine and flip through the pages.

The right listing photos will have the same effect on your potential tenants. Eye-catching photos will encourage them to click on your listing. If they like what they see, you're one step closer to bringing them on as tenants.

After all, your potential tenants will be scrolling through dozens of different listings as they search for their new residence. If you want to stand out from the crowd, you need photos that show off your property's incredible features and allow your potential tenants to envision themselves living there.

Some real estate investors prefer to hire a professional photographer for their listing photos. Others do it themselves. Choose the right approach for your needs and budget. A high-quality camera is helpful if you want top-of-the-line photos, but many people can also get great results with a camera phone with a little practice and patience.

If you decide to take the photos yourself, here's how to make sure they capture your dream tenant's attention:

- **Consider staging the home:** Yes, you can take listing photos of an empty home. But vacant rooms tend to look smaller and less inviting, which is the exact opposite of what you're aiming for. Stage your photos with simple furniture and décor, or work with a staging company to set up your property for the photos.
- **Make it seem like home:** Add some fresh flowers and decorative features to each room to make it seem lived in. The decor doesn't need to be flashy but should make the unit feel like a home.
- **Use natural light:** Pick a sunny day and open the windows to feature the home in its best light. Artificial and flash photography can make the photos look dull instead of bright and inviting.

- **Make it seem spacious:** Use a tripod and set it up in the doorway of the room to give viewers a clear picture of the entire room. Set up your camera at various heights and take several photos to give yourself options for the listing.
- **Don't forget the details:** If the home has beautiful details, like a cozy fireplace or hidden storage nooks, snap some photos to highlight them. These elements can help increase the home's value in the eyes of your potential tenant.
- **Make editing easy:** Take tons of photos so you have plenty of options to choose from when you compile your listing. When you take photos, make sure the camera is straight and that you leave room to crop photos as needed.

As your real estate portfolio grows, you'll become an expert at taking amazing listing photos. Keep practicing, and don't be afraid to reshoot photos when tenants move out or you relist the unit.

Where to List

You have your rental price. You have your photos. Now it's time to actually list the property. After all, your dream tenants aren't going to find you by chance!

There are a lot of rental platforms out there, and each one has its pros and cons. I will break down three of the most popular ones to help you find the best option for you.

Apartments.com

When tenants look for a new place to live, Apartments.com is often one of their first stops, making it an excellent place to list your property. They've invested a lot of money into marketing the platform so tenants know and trust them.

They can also help you manage the property once you find a tenant. You can conduct tenant screenings, collect rent, and manage maintenance requests through Apartments.com.

There are fees associated with some of the features on Apartments.com. For instance, you can upgrade to a premium listing for a fee. This website also charges for tenant screenings and includes a transaction fee for rent payments.

Facebook

If you want to find renters without opening your wallet, Facebook is a great option. With over two billion daily users, it is the best way to get your rental property in front of as many people as possible.

You'll need a Facebook account to set up your listing, and you'll want to include all relevant details and photos in your description.

Facebook is an excellent way to generate leads for your property, but you'll need to be prepared to field messages and have a system in place to vet potential renters. It's also not a one-stop shop, so you'll need a process for setting up showings, preparing leases, and collecting rental payments.

Zillow Rental Manager

Like Apartments.com, Zillow offers a one-stop shop for landlords. You can list your property for free on the platform, which has over 30 million visitors each month between Zillow, Trulia, and HotPads. It also offers tenant screenings, a lease builder, and a rent collection tool.

Zillow Rental Manager allows you to list your rental for free, but you'll need to upgrade to premium to truly stand out from the crowd. You also need to be careful using Zillow's data since it can be inaccurate.

Research, as always, is your friend when it comes to finding places to list your rental. Try some traditional listing methods like the ones listed above, and experiment with other up-and-comers until you find the approach that works best for you. Try posting your listing on local Reddit forums, Craigslist, and other social media platforms. Build an email list or social media account and update your audience about vacancies. Connect with other local businesses that can recommend your property to new employees. Remember, your goal is to make it easy for your prospective tenants to find you.

How to Screen Tenants

You've posted your listing and received your first inquiry from a potential tenant. Hooray! It's exciting to learn someone is interested in renting your property. But that doesn't mean you should hand over the keys to them just yet.

You want to make sure the tenant will be able to pay the rent each month and treat your property with respect. The tenant screening portion of the rental process is incredibly important because it's your chance to vet the potential renter thoroughly. Just like you performed your due diligence before buying your property, you need to perform due diligence on anyone who wants to rent from you.

What Questions to Ask Potential Tenants

You'll have the chance to ask tenants questions multiple times throughout the application process. Many landlords have screening questionnaires that potential renters complete at the start of the inquiry process. These questionnaires help the landlord determine whether the potential tenant is a genuine lead or not.

You will also have the opportunity to talk with potential renters when you show them the property or during a phone call.

Before you develop a screening questionnaire or talk with a potential tenant, sit down and write down all the questions you'd like to have answered. Some of these questions might include:

- When do you plan to move?
- How do you generate an income?
- Do you have any pets?
- Do you or any other potential tenants smoke?
- Have you ever been convinced of a crime?

Some of these questions might be uncomfortable to ask, but they are necessary. After all, your property is a big investment. You want to make sure that your tenants can meet their financial obligations and treat your property with respect.

When you prepare your questions, avoid any that could be considered discriminatory. Federal law protects people from discrimination. Do not ask questions or make comments pertaining to:

- Race
- National origin
- Color
- Gender
- Religion
- Marital Status
- Disabilities

If you ask any experienced landlord, their list of tenant screening questions is probably very different than when they started. You'll find that your list of screening questions also evolves as you become more experienced as a landlord.

How to Conduct a Background Check and Credit Check

Running a background and credit check on a potential tenant is non-negotiable for landlords. You want a trustworthy, reliable tenant. Taking the time to vet them thoroughly will reduce the risk of tenant-related headaches later.

To run a background check, you need written consent from the tenant. You can add this to your rental application or send it separately.

Then, you need to collect the information needed to run the check. You should ask for the date of birth and social security number of anyone who will be living in the house. You'll also need two previous addresses and the name of their employer.

Finally, use a background check service to complete the check. There are various options available, so check with other investors to find the ones they recommend. You can run background checks through services like RentPrep and E-Renter, among others.

To pull your potential tenant's credit report, use a service like Experian, TransUnion, or Equifax. You can also hire a tenant-specific agency. RentPrep also offers a credit check service.

Helpful Hints for Screening Tenants

Conducting background checks and asking plenty of screening questions will help you find reliable tenants, but you shouldn't stop there. I've learned over the years that there are other steps you can take to improve your screening process. Learn from my experience and take these steps to optimize your screening process:

- **Know your own personal screening requirements:** Decide what your ideal tenant's income, credit score, and required references are. Also, decide whether you will allow tenants with pets or children (some landlords won't rent to pet owners and some prefer the 55+ age group). Finalize these requirements before you list your property.
- **Use screening applications to your advantage:** Collect basic information like names, addresses, smoking, and pet information in your first communication with a potential renter, preferably through a form. This will reduce the amount of time you spend talking with unqualified applicants
- **Learn and adjust:** Don't be afraid to adjust your process as you learn more about the market and the real estate business. You might learn you need to ask for more references or lower your criteria for income. Follow the data, and don't be afraid to pivot as you grow.

What to Know About Tenant Applications

You've pored over tenant applications, run your background and credit checks, and intensely vetted every potential tenant. Now, it's decision time.

Perhaps you've narrowed the pool to two or three prospective tenants, or maybe you have just one finalist. Either way, you're in the final stretch of the selection process.

Showing the Property

Your tenants will likely want to see the property in person before signing a lease. Showing a property is a multi-step process that begins before the tenant ever pulls into the driveway. Before you have an in-person showing, you'll want to:

- **Schedule an appointment with the prospective tenant:** Set up a date and time to meet with the potential renter at the property. Make sure you leave yourself enough time to get to the property beforehand and make sure it's up to par. If you're doing multiple showings in one day, leave a buffer zone so tenants aren't running into each other between appointments.
- **Clean the property:** Inspect the property before the potential tenants arrive to make sure it is clean and looks well-maintained. Empty the trash, spray air freshener, tidy the yard, and verify that the property looks pristine.
- **Have a safety plan:** Even if your potential tenant seems great, you still don't know them. Make sure you meet in broad daylight and let someone you trust know where you are going and how long you expect the tour to last.

When it's time to meet the tenant and show the property, make sure you put your best foot—and the property's best foot—forward. Make a great first impression by:

- **Dressing professionally:** You don't have to wear a full suit, but be sure to look presentable.
- **Being prepared:** Your potential tenants will have questions about the history of the property, the neighborhood, and the surrounding area. Do some research and game plan how you will answer potential questions.
- **Treating it like a business meeting:** Whether this is your first property or your fifth, real estate investing is your business. Treat it like you would any other business meeting. Shake your prospective tenant's hand, be on time, and act like you would in the workplace.

After you've talked with the tenant, showed them the property, highlighted its features, and answered their questions, you'll probably have a hunch about whether they'll be interested in signing a lease—and whether they're the right tenant for your property. Set a time and date to follow up and make sure you reach out.

How to Approve or Deny a Potential Tenant

When you follow up with a potential applicant, you'll learn whether they are still interested in the property. The final decision to offer a lease agreement, though, falls solely on you. You have the power to approve or deny a tenant.

If they have pets, you can charge a pet deposit and a monthly pet fee to cover wear and tear. Make sure these additional fees are aligned with local practices.

If the tenant meets your desired requirements for a renter and wants to move forward, let them know they've been approved and send them the lease agreement. This lease agreement should be thorough and include addendums and clauses to protect you, the tenant, and the property for the duration of the lease agreement. A lawyer can review your lease before you send it over to confirm you didn't miss anything.

Unfortunately, sometimes a potential tenant just isn't the right fit. If this happens, politely let them know that you've denied the application. Hold firm to your criteria and make sure you apply the same criteria to every potential tenant.

How to Collect a Security Deposit

When you and your tenant agree to the lease, you can collect a security deposit. If you've ever rented a house or apartment, you are likely familiar with this process.

A security deposit is a predetermined amount of money you hold on to for the duration of the lease. If the tenant damages the property, you can use the security deposit to pay for the damages. If there are no damages when the tenant moves out, you must return the security deposit to them. In most states, a security deposit should not exceed one month's rent.

You can adjust the security deposit based on factors like the tenant's credit score or expected income. For example, you might ask for a higher security deposit from a tenant with pets or unreliable income, or a reduced security deposit to entice a tenant with an excellent credit score to sign the lease.

Outline the terms and conditions for the security deposit in the lease. Always collect it before handing over the keys to the property.

How to Write a Lease That Protects You

A lease is a contract between you and the tenant. It specifies what you will give them (access to a property) and what they will give you (the rental payment). It also details stipulations that you will be required to follow as the landlord and that the tenant will be required to follow as the renter.

Before you draw up a lease for your property, there are a few things you must consider, starting with the lease terms.

Month-to-Month vs. Long-Term Leases

When you create a lease, you have the power to determine how long the lease will last. A month-to-month lease renews every 30 days unless it is terminated by you or the tenant. A long-term lease has a set duration for the terms. Some popular options include three months, six months, or 12 months. In a long-term lease, you and the tenant lock in the rent price for a specific amount of time. If a tenant breaks the lease early, you can collect a penalty outlined in the lease.

A month-to-month lease is helpful for tenants who need flexible housing. You can charge a premium price for a month-to-month lease, but you'll have to accept that the tenant might leave the agreement at any time, leaving you with a vacancy.

A long-term lease provides stability for you and the tenant. The tradeoff is that you'll likely have to charge a little less for rent than for a month-to-month lease, and you won't be able to raise rates to meet market value for the duration of the lease.

How to Get a Lease Contract

I strongly, strongly recommend you seek help from a professional to prepare your leasing agreement. This document is crucial to your business, and it's worth investing in. The lease is your opportunity to lay out your expectations for tenants for payment and cancellation. It also lets you set guidelines for the tenant's responsibilities for maintaining the property and lays out what will happen if your property is damaged. Trust me, this is not a document you want to throw together at the last minute.

You have several options for creating the lease, including:

- **Hiring an attorney:** A licensed attorney with real estate experience can draw up a lease that covers all your bases. Ask for recommendations from other real estate investors and do your own research before selecting an attorney.
- **Generating the document online:** Sites like Zillow Rental Manager offer free lease templates you can update for your property. If you use this option, make sure your lease meets all the necessary state requirements.
- **Check with local associations:** If your area has a professional association for realtors, landlords, and attorneys, check to see if they offer free lease templates. These documents will align with your state requirements and can be a great starting point for creating a lease.

What to Include in a Lease

You can—and should—adapt your lease to each of your properties. But regardless of how you adapt your lease, every version should include:

- **Contact information:** Your lease should include contact information for you, the tenant(s), and, if applicable, the property manager. Each party should provide their full name, mailing address, phone number, and email address.
- **Property details:** Property details include the address and a list of anything provided with the property, like appliances or furniture.

- **Utility payment details:** Will you pay the utilities or the tenant? Outline expectations in the lease, including if there are required utility providers for the property.
- **Duration and payment terms:** Include how long the lease will last, the amount due for rent each month, how rent should be paid, and the due date. Be specific about when rent is considered late and what happens if you don't receive payment.
- **Termination and eviction terms:** Outline the procedure and expectations for terminating the lease and the process for eviction.
- **Insurance requirements:** Research the insurance requirements in your state and include the details in the lease. If your tenants are required to have renter's insurance, describe the type and amount of coverage they need in this section of the lease.
- **Property policies:** Lay out the policies for smoking, pets, parking, and guests. If there is a pet fee or an additional charge for more parking spaces, specify that in the lease.
- **Rules and expectations:** Does the tenant dispose of trash, or do you handle it? Will they plow the driveway and maintain the yard, or is landscape maintenance provided? Be clear about what the tenant needs to do to maintain the property and describe what you will handle as the landlord.

As you can see, your lease should be a very specific document. This is the time to decide what you expect from a tenant and lay it out clearly. Take the time to write a lease that is clear, thorough, and all-encompassing. It will save you time down the road.

Signing the Lease

Your lease is complete. Now it's time to sign the paperwork and hand the keys over to your new tenant.

After you've approved the tenant and they're ready to move forward, send over an unsigned lease and set a deadline for its return. Give them enough time—usually several days—to review the agreement before they sign it.

Once the tenant has reviewed the lease and signed it, they'll send it back to you. Once you sign the lease, it is binding. Print out a copy to save for your records and provide a copy to the tenant for their records. If issues arise, refer back to the lease agreement to determine how to proceed.

TENANT MANAGEMENT

The day has finally arrived. Your tenant is officially moving into your rental property and their new home. It's exciting, but your work as a landlord is not done, especially if you decide not to hire a property manager.

Tenant management is an ongoing process. In this section, we'll go over various aspects of keeping your tenants happy, your property protected, and the rent checks rolling in.

Move In

When a tenant moves into your rental, excitement is at an all-time high for both of you. The tenant is filled with expectations about their life in your rental unit, from cozy dinners in the breakfast nook to watching TV in the living room. You might also have some visions of your own, like a quiet tenant and perfectly maintained property.

As a landlord, move-in day is a chance to welcome the tenant to your property and set expectations for how the tenant-landlord relationship will unfold. Your move-in process should include two key components: an inspection and a welcome packet.

Move-In Inspection

Before your tenant arrives, complete a walkthrough of the property. Check every room in the house for damage. Make sure the appliances, plumbing, and electrical systems are working properly. Check the garage and yard for signs of damage or wear and tear. Take videos or photos to record the state of the property before the tenant moves in.

When the tenant arrives, walk through the property again with them or provide them with a checklist to walk through it themselves. Note any damage, big or small, on the property. When you are finished with the inspection, you and the tenant should sign the checklist.

This process allows you and the tenant to get on the same page about the condition of the property. If the tenant notices an issue, you can develop a plan to address it. It also prepares you for the move-out process, whenever that may be. If there is damage to the property when the tenant moves out, you can hold them accountable according to the terms of the lease.

Welcome Packet

The welcome packet is your chance to provide necessary information about the property to your tenants as well as welcome them to the area. This packet should be robust and include everything they need to know about their new residence.

Make sure you include basic paperwork in the welcome packet, including a copy of the lease, contact information for you or the property manager, and the move-in inspection checklist. Outline the procedures for paying rent and requesting repairs or maintenance, as well as the rules for the property.

You'll also want to provide everything your tenant needs to access the home, including several copies of the keys, remote door openers, and information about access codes if there is a security system.

If you want to go above and beyond, welcome the tenant to the area with a map of the city and a list of local establishments. Some landlords choose to provide a small gift, like a gift card to a local pizza shop or a bottle of wine, to welcome tenants to the rental. It's a small touch, but it can help start your relationship with the tenants on the right foot.

Rent Collection

Let's be real: you're not investing in real estate out of the goodness of your heart. You're running a business, and you need to get paid. There are a few ways to collect rent, including by cash or check. If you want to make the process incredibly easy, though, you need to set up an online rent collection process.

Most of your tenants will expect to pay their rent online. It's a win-win for you and the tenant. You'll receive your payments quickly and on time, and your tenants won't have to worry about waiting for a check to clear or missing a payment.

To collect rent online, you can use a bank transfer or a collection software system. Zillow Rental Manager and Apartments.com offer rent collection services. You can also be paid via Venmo, PayPal, or Apple Pay. You can also set up a process for collecting rent via credit card.

What If Your Tenants Don't Pay?

It's the second of the month, and your tenant still hasn't paid rent. It's officially late. Now what?

When a tenant doesn't pay rent on time, they are violating their lease and breaching the contract both of you signed. When this happens, it's best to start with the basics.

Before you contact your tenant, check your records and bank account one more time. Make sure the payment hasn't been processed. After all, everyone makes mistakes—it's possible you missed the payment when you were reviewing your accounts.

If the tenant is indeed late, it's time to create a paper trail. Send them a notice about the missed payment and let them know about next steps. If the missed payment was an oversight, the tenant will pay it and the late fee, and you'll both be able to move forward. If you still don't receive payment, you can try to call the tenant. Do not call more than once, though. The phone call is a courtesy. Multiple calls will feel like harassment, which you want to avoid.

If you still don't receive payment, it's time to start the eviction process. Begin by sending an official document called a pay or quit notice, which should clearly state the next steps. Tell the tenant that you plan to evict if you are not paid in full, including late fees. Set a deadline for receiving payment.

After you've posted the pay or quit notice, find a lawyer with experience in evictions. Depending on your state, you can start the eviction process after several days of nonpayment following the pay or quit notice. Your lawyer can guide you through the specific steps of the eviction process in your state.

Listen, I know that waiting on rent payments can be frustrating. The longer you wait to receive the money that is owed to you, the angrier you become. If you find yourself in this situation, the best advice I can give you is to be patient, stay calm, get as much as you can in writing, and seek the help of an experienced eviction lawyer. The eviction process can take time, but trust that it will work out in your favor. Don't let it keep you from moving forward with real estate investing.

Grace Periods and Extensions

We've all fallen on tough financial times, and your tenants might experience hardships while renting from you. There are a few ways to handle these situations so that your tenant can meet their obligations to you. The most popular options are grace periods and extensions.

Grace Periods

Grace periods are extremely common in the rental world. Some states require them, and others leave it up to the landlord's discretion. A grace period is just what it sounds like—an extra cushion that gives tenants a few extra days to pay rent. For example, though rent is due on the first of the month, it isn't considered late until the fifth. Those extra few days are the grace period.

If you provide a grace period, you need to include the details of it in the lease agreement. When does the grace period end? What is the late fee? These details ensure that you and the tenant are clear about the expectations for payment.

A grace period protects you and the tenant. Things happen, and sometimes bank transfers are delayed due to errors or holidays. A grace period gives your tenant time to pay their rent without being assessed a fee and helps you maintain your relationship with the tenant.

Rent Extension

If your tenant falls on particularly hard times, like a job loss or other financial hardship, they may ask for a rent extension. Granting an extension can help you maintain the relationship and retain the tenant. If they are a reliable tenant, you might decide it is worth it to give them some extra time to come up with their payment.

If you decide to grant a tenant an extension, detail the conversation in writing and lay out the terms for payment. Consider asking for a partial rent payment along with additional installments until the rent is paid in full.

If you don't feel comfortable granting an extension, don't. Use your judgment.

Communicating with Tenants

Ideally, you won't need to communicate much with your tenants. Hopefully, they pay their rent on time, rarely request repairs, and adhere to the terms of your lease.

But we don't live in a perfect world. Chances are, you'll have to chat with your tenants in some capacity, whether it's to set up a maintenance appointment or discuss lease renewals. You can vary your method of communication based on the topic.

Email

Email is an excellent option for tenant communication because it provides a paper trail for your interactions with the client. It's an easy way to share paperwork or general announcements about the property without interrupting the tenant's daily life.

If you plan to use email to communicate with tenants, have a system in place to remind you to follow up when needed. It's easy for an important email to get lost in someone's inbox. Be sure you're ready to follow up via another email or escalate the conversation to a phone call or text message if necessary.

Texting

Texting is a great way to communicate with tenants, but you'll need some boundaries in place to keep your phone from buzzing at all hours of the day and night. If you decide to use texting to connect with tenants, ask for their consent when they move in. Let them know what you will share with them via text, and try not to text them beyond business hours.

Texting should be used for specific circumstances. Text messages are great for reminding tenants about upcoming maintenance or rent payments. They are not ideal for in-depth conversations with tenants.

Phone Call

Phone calls should be used for urgent matters that are best discussed face-to-face (or voice-to-voice). Let tenants know that they can call you if there is an emergency on the property, but specify what you consider an emergency. Let them know how quickly they should expect a response from you if you miss their call.

Keep in mind that phone calls are not ideal for legal conversations because you can't document them. If you think you'll need to revisit details about the conversation later, try to conduct it through email, mail, or text message so you have documentation of the interaction.

Written Notice

Sometimes, you need to communicate with a tenant the old-fashioned way: on paper. For example, if you offer the tenant a lease renewal, you might send them details via email and follow up with a letter through the mail outlining the details for their personal records.

How to Handle Maintenance and Repairs

As a landlord, you have a responsibility to provide a livable environment for your tenants. It's up to you to respond to maintenance requests and complete repairs in a timely manner. It's good for business and your reputation.

Some maintenance tasks, like changing batteries in the smoke alarm, are the tenant's responsibility. The rest falls on your shoulders, and tenants won't hesitate to reach out when something needs to be fixed.

And here's the thing—as annoying as an unexpected maintenance request can be, it's a good thing when a tenant lets you know something is wrong with your property. It gives you a chance to fix it, keep your tenant happy, and maintain the value of your property. That's a win-win for everyone involved.

It will be easier to handle maintenance requests efficiently if you have a process in place. Here's what to consider as you design your process:

- **How should tenants submit requests?** You need one streamlined way for tenants to let you know when the property needs maintenance or repairs. Decide if you want them to communicate with you via text, email, or an online application.
- **How will you organize repairs and maintenance?** You need to track every request received, document how you addressed each one, and monitor the cost of repairs. Try setting up a spreadsheet to get you started.
- **How will you confirm the issue has been resolved?** You'll want to follow up with the tenant via email, text, or an online application to confirm the issue has been addressed and officially close the request.
- **What is considered an emergency?** In the case of a true emergency, like a busted AC unit in the summer or a major plumbing issue, you'll want your tenants to reach out to you immediately. Decide what constitutes an emergency and let the tenant know to call you if an emergency occurs. Detail these expectations in the welcome packet when they move in.

I hate to break it to you, but chances are these maintenance issues will arise at really inconvenient times. It can be easy to delay addressing them if you are busy with something else. I encourage you to avoid procrastinating when it comes to handling maintenance requests from tenants. Addressing these issues quickly strengthens the tenant-landlord relationship and makes it more likely that the tenant will renew when their lease expires.

Always acknowledge maintenance requests and try to provide a timeline for repairs. Try to address urgent issues, like a broken washing machine, within 24-48 hours. Non-urgent issues, like a squeaky stair, can be addressed within a week or two.

How to Reduce Expenses and Increase Your Income

Your goal for every single property you own should be to maximize your profits. There are plenty of ways to do this without cutting corners or inconveniencing your tenants.

As you generate cash flow, you might want to reinvest those funds into the property. This helps you in two ways: it increases the value of your property, and it provides a better experience for tenants. Some investments you can make to cut costs and maximize your income include:

- **Making the property energy-efficient:** Consider upgrading your heating or cooling system to a more energy-efficient model or swapping out appliances for updated versions.
- **Learn maintenance skills:** The more repairs you can do yourself, the more money you'll save on maintenance costs. Take some time to learn basic maintenance tasks and enjoy the extra cash in your pocket.
- **Reevaluate the landscaping:** Could you swap grass for turf and eliminate the need for a lawn care service? Consider making some adjustments to the landscape to cut costs.
- **Examine your plumbing:** If you are paying the water bill, try switching out shower heads and calibrating toilets so they use water more efficiently.

If you want to reduce your expenses and maximize your income, you should also focus on keeping your tenants happy, especially if they are your ideal renters. When a tenant leaves, you have to invest money into finding and screening a new tenant and making the property move-in ready. Build a good relationship with your tenant, address their maintenance needs quickly, and communicate as needed. If you do these things, they'll be more likely to renew their lease when the time comes.

How to Handle Common Tenant Issues

It's impossible to plan for every tenant issue you'll encounter as a real estate investor. There are some issues, however, that tend to pop up no matter what. Here are three common problems and guidance on how to handle each one:

Tenant Issue #1: "There are bugs in this house!"

Pests want the pleasures of home, too. If ants and other pests have taken up residence in your rental, your tenants will let you know about it. When this happens, head out to the property as soon as possible to evaluate the extent of the issue. Develop a plan for exterminating the critters and share it with your tenants. Hire an exterminator and make sure the problem is taken care of thoroughly.

Tenant Issue #2: "The neighbors are making too much noise!"

If you are renting out both sides of a duplex, you might encounter this complaint and be able to do something about it. In most cases, a short conversation with the person complaining about the noise will help you address the root of the issue. Then, you can have a short conversation with the noisy neighbor and ask them to be more considerate. If it's a continuous problem, address it based on the terms laid out in the lease. If you don't have a noise complaint clause in the lease, consider adding one.

Tenant Issue #3: "I want my security deposit back!"

When a tenant moves out, you'll have the opportunity to review the property for damages. If there is damage, you can keep the security deposit. Some tenants are not happy about this. If they ask for their deposit back, refer back to the photos and checklist from move-in and highlight where the damage has occurred. In some cases, this can evolve into a legal issue, so consult an attorney if things escalate.

What to Know About the Fair Housing Act

The Fair Housing Act protects renters from discrimination. As a landlord, it is your responsibility to understand the Fair Housing Act and other protections granted to renters in your state.

The Fair Housing Act protects people from discrimination based on race, color, religion, national origin, familial status, sex, and disability. Some states have additional protections, like age or sexual orientation.

In order to stay compliant, you need to be very careful about how you communicate in all aspects of your rental business. For example, if you state a preference for female renters in your rental listing, that can be a violation of the Fair Housing Act.

This principle also applies to questions you ask potential tenants during the screening process. For instance, asking a potential tenant where they go to church could be considered a violation of the Fair Housing Act.

How to Streamline Your Property

As you add more rental properties to your portfolio, you'll be desperate to start streamlining your operations as much as possible.

Why wait? Whether you have one property or several, it's never too early to start incorporating the newest technology into your rentals. Here are three ways to upgrade your rental and make your life a little bit easier.

Smart Locks

A smart lock makes physical keys a thing of the past—or at least keeps them buried in your pocket or purse. Adding a keyless entry system is a great way to upgrade your locks and make life easier for you and your tenants.

Smart locks provide easy access for tenants, regardless of whether they have their physical keys with them or not. For landlords, smart locks are a game-changer for security and tenant transitions. If you have smart locks on your property, you can provide different codes for service providers, maintenance companies, and tenants. When someone enters the code, you'll be notified.

Smart locks are more expensive to install, but they will help you save money in the long run. One of the biggest benefits comes when tenants move out. Instead of changing the locks on every door in the property, you can simply switch out the code for the new tenants.

Smart Thermostat

If you (or your tenants) dread opening the electric bill every month, it might be time to install a smart thermostat. Smart thermostats automatically adjust the temperature in the house based on your schedule. It's connected to the Wi-Fi in the home and allows the user to control the thermostat remotely.

Smart thermostats are popular in short and mid-term rentals because the landlord often foots the electric bill. A smart thermostat gives the landlord some control over the temperature in the house, allowing them to reduce costs.

For long-term rentals, tenants are typically covering the electric bill. As a result, a smart thermostat is a money-saving perk for tenants. Having one in your rental might be an extra incentive that keeps tenants happy and makes them more likely to renew.

Smart Safety Devices

One of your biggest responsibilities as a landlord is to keep your property and tenants safe. Thanks to technology, there are now more devices than ever to monitor your rental.

You might want to consider investing in a Ring camera or another security device to protect your property. Ring cameras can be a deterrent to crime. After all, no thief wants to be caught on camera!

It can also provide a sense of security to your tenants. Having the extra layer of security a Ring camera provides can make your tenants feel more comfortable at home. It might even be the feature that sets your rental property apart from others.

How to Remove Tenants

We talked a bit about evictions earlier in this chapter. Now, we'll explore how and when to remove tenants in more detail.

There are several reasons you might need to evict or remove a tenant, including:

- **Failing to pay rent:** As discussed earlier, if a tenant habitually pays rent late or doesn't pay at all, you can remove them.
- **Damaging the property:** If a tenant intentionally destroys your property or allows gross negligence to occur, you can pursue removing them from the rental.
- **Using the property for illegal activities:** If you can prove that your tenant is participating in illegal activity on your property, you can remove them.
- **Violating the lease:** If a tenant has an unauthorized pet or participates in an activity that violates the terms of the lease, you can pursue removing them from the property.

There are two common ways to remove tenants: cash for keys and eviction. Let's take a closer look at both of them.

Eviction

Evicting a tenant is a lengthy process. No landlord wants to do it, but sometimes it is necessary. Hopefully, this is a rare occurrence throughout your real estate career.

If you do end up deciding to evict a tenant, here's how to do it:

- **Review the law:** Check the laws for your state or consult an attorney before moving forward with an eviction. Different states and municipalities have different landlord-tenant laws. You want to be sure you can win.
- **Consider alternatives:** Evictions are expensive and stressful, even for landlords. Ask the tenant if they want to

leave the property on their own or offer them a cash-for-keys exchange, which will be discussed in the next section.

- **Serve the eviction notice:** The type of notice depends on the violation. A pay or quit notice is used when a tenant owes unpaid rent. A cure or quit notice is used if a tenant is in violation of the lease, but can fix the problem by removing an unauthorized pet or roommate. An unconditional quit notice is used when the tenant needs to vacate immediately due to illegal activity or gross negligence. If the tenant doesn't take the necessary action to address the notice, it's time to move on to the next step.
- **File a lawsuit:** Hire an attorney to file your eviction suit and walk you through the process. An eviction lawyer will know exactly what you need to file in your state.
- **Gather your documents:** Your attorney can advise you on what paperwork you will need to bring to court for your hearing. In most cases, you will need the original lease agreement, documents related to the eviction, and copies of any communication you had with the tenant.
- **Complete the eviction:** If you win in court, local law enforcement will receive a Writ of Restitution. Then, they will go to the property and remove the tenant. You will also receive a financial judgment. The judgment typically requires the evictee to pay the rent you are owed and additional damages.

See? It's a lengthy, tedious process. Thankfully, it's not the only way to remove a tenant.

Cash for Keys

Cash for keys is an alternative to an eviction. In a cash-for-keys exchange, the landlord pays the tenant an agreed-upon fee to vacate the property.

I know what you're thinking—why on earth would any landlord pay a bad tenant? I get it, but there's a method to the madness.

Landlords tend to use this option because it is more time and cost-efficient. As you saw earlier, evictions can be costly and time-consuming. A cash-for-keys exchange allows landlords to avoid this process and remove the tenant faster than going through the legal eviction process. It also typically saves them money.

If you decide to pursue a cash-for-keys exchange, you will need to:

- **Serve an eviction notice:** Research the eviction process in your state and serve the appropriate notice. You aren't legally required to serve an eviction notice, but it can help you in the negotiation process.
- **Make a verbal offer:** Talk with your tenant to see if they'd be open to a cash-for-keys exchange. Discuss the dollar amount and the move-out date.
- **Put it in writing:** If the tenant agrees, send them a written contract. Hire an attorney to help with this if possible.
- **Finalize the exchange:** Sign the documents and exchange the keys and cash. Conduct a move-out inspection, wave goodbye to your tenant, and move on.

Whether you choose to evict or use cash for keys, removing a tenant is never fun. If you find yourself in this situation, use it as a learning opportunity for your business. Review your application and background check process. Consider adjusting your income and credit score criteria for your next tenant. Don't dwell on this chapter of your real estate career—use it to make the next chapter even better.

Moving Out

All good things must come to an end. Eventually, your tenant will move on to a new city or a new property. When that time comes, you want to have a clearly defined move-out process to ensure your tenant can exit the property quickly and smoothly. Also, you'll want to ensure you can recoup any potential costs for damages or repairs and can quickly prep the property for your next tenant. This process isn't lengthy, but does require several key components.

Move-Out Packet

The move-out packet provides all the information your tenant needs to leave the property, from cleaning guidelines to instructions for inspections. Most move-out checklists include:

- **Confirmation of the move-out date:** Reiterate when the tenant is supposed to exit the property. Include the date and time (for example, by midnight on April 1).
- **Forwarding information:** The tenant should provide a way to reach them via phone, email, and mail.
- **Inspection details:** Let the tenant know how to schedule their move-out inspection and any details about what to expect during the process.
- **Cleaning instructions:** Outline how the tenant should leave the property. For example, you might ask them to sweep, dispose of trash, wipe down the walls, clean out the fridge, clean the carpets, remove pet waste from the yard, etc.
- **Utility guidelines:** Let the tenant know how long they must keep utilities on. In many instances, utilities should remain on until after the move-out date.
- **Key return details:** Outline when and how the tenant will hand over the keys to the property.

Move-Out Inspection

The move-out inspection is your opportunity to walk through the property with the tenant and check for damage. Now's the time to pull out the move-in inspection checklist you created when the tenant arrived at the property, including photos. You can use the move-in checklist to compare the condition of the property at move-out to the condition at move-in.

During the inspection, you should look for damage that exceeds normal wear and tear. Normal wear and tear include things like reasonable scratches on the walls, worn carpet, and nail holes. This type of damage is reasonable for any space that has been lived in. Remember, your property was the tenant's home, so it is reasonable for them to have hung photographs on the walls or walked on the carpet.

However, damage can sometimes exceed what is reasonable. In these circumstances, you can use the security deposit to cover the repairs. This damage is called tenant property damage and can include large holes in the walls, broken windows, torn window screens, or missing fixtures. If you spot tenant property damage, notify the tenant during the inspection. In many cases, the security deposit will cover the repairs. If not, estimate the total cost of repairs or, if appropriate, give them the opportunity to fix the damage.

Returning the Deposit

If you complete the move-out inspection, it's time to return the security deposit. If there has been some level of tenant property damage, you might need to use some of the security deposit to repair the damage. In this scenario, you will need to create documentation about how much of the deposit you are keeping and why. This document should include tenant information, a description of the damage, the amount needed to repair the damage, and the amount of the security deposit the tenant will receive after deductions.

If there is no property damage, you need to return the security deposit in full to the tenant. Check your state and local laws for guidance on how to approach this process. Many states have specific time frames for when you must return the deposit.

If property damage exceeds the amount of the security deposit, you may need to take legal action if the tenant is unwilling to cover the costs.

Preparing the Unit for the Next Tenant

After the tenant moves out, it's time to prepare the property for your next move-in. Before your next tenant moves in, be sure to:

- Repaint the walls
- Change all locks and make new sets of keys
- Clean the property thoroughly

- Complete any necessary repairs
- Take updated photos of the property

CONTRACTORS

Real estate investing might seem like a solo endeavor, but it is not. You need a network of reliable contractors to help you repair and maintain your property. These extremely skilled workers will help keep your properties in tip-top shape.

How to Find Good Contractors

The process of finding good contractors is similar to building any other type of network. You need to ask for recommendations, check references, and understand the exact type of skills you need for each project. When asking for recommendations, make sure contractors are skilled in the area you need help in. For example, not all landscaping companies do masonry repairs on walkways because their skills may apply only to lawn care.

Ask other real estate inventors and realtors for recommendations. Take note of any work trucks you see in your neighborhood and ask other homeowners for recommendations. As you start to hire contractors, ask them for recommendations as well. Your favorite plumber might know an excellent carpenter and vice versa.

Once you have a list of potential contractors, check their references. Call previous clients to see what they think of their work and search for the company name online to see if there are any reviews. You should also check that contracts have appropriate licenses and insurance policies, if applicable. Check online reviews. What's most important with reviews is how they handle negative reviews. Did they ignore them? Respond with a half-hearted apology? Or, did they respond professionally and demonstrate genuine concern for the customer's satisfaction? Everyone makes mistakes, and some people like to leave bad reviews just because they're angry people. So, focus more on the contractor's response than the review itself—unless there are consistently bad reviews, in which case, don't hire this individual or company.

Eventually, you'll have a list of several contractors to speak with. Determine exactly what you need to be done for your project and pick up the phone. Ask them for a price estimate, and be sure to shop around to compare costs and timelines.

How to Manage Contractors

Your role does not end when you hire a contractor. Just like you, contractors are running a business, which means they have their own project requirements, timelines, and costs to think about.

There should be a contract in place before work begins. Make sure you read and thoroughly understand the contract before you sign it. The contract should include specifics about the project timeline, expected costs, and details on other aspects of the project, like using subcontractors. This part of the process is your opportunity to outline your expectations for the project and get on the same page with the contractor.

When work begins, your contractor might have questions about the project or other tasks you need to complete, like acquiring permits. Have an established process for communication in place, and do your best to respond promptly. Communication is key to completing projects on time. Prioritize it!

Tip: always hire contractors or handymen who hold professional liability insurance. You are running a business, so hire professionals who carry the necessary insurance for your protection (in the case of injury) or property damage.

Why You Need a Handyman on Speed Dial

Sometimes, you don't need a specialist to complete a home repair project. While a plumber, carpenter, or electrician can help you with high-level home projects, a handyman can handle some other projects.

A highly skilled handyman can complete a lot of detailed home improvement tasks, like repairing a deck or installing cabinetry. In some cases, these projects might be things you could learn to do yourself, but hiring a handyman saves you valuable time. From fixing a faucet to replacing a window, a great handyman can tackle your to-do list quickly. They also tend to charge a daily or hourly rate, while a contractor typically charges by the project.

Licensed vs. Unlicensed

A handyman is a great option for many home projects because the tasks they complete don't require specific licenses. An unlicensed handyman can still complete basic repairs.

On the other hand, you will most likely want to hire a licensed contractor for in-depth projects. Most states require licenses for contractors, electricians, plumbers, and HVAC installers. Confirming a contractor is licensed helps protect you from scams. As you meet other real estate investors, you will likely hear horror stories about contractors who performed shoddy work or took a customer's money and never completed the project. In many cases, you'll learn that these contractors were not licensed.

Using an unlicensed contractor can lead to issues with permits, safety issues, and damages to your property. Before you hire a contractor, ask for their licensing information and confirm that it's up to date on your state's licensing website.

As previously mentioned, make sure anyone working on your property is well-insured so you're not left holding the tab for property damage they caused while on the job.

How to Screen a Contractor

You should always speak with your potential contractor before hiring them for your project. In addition to personally checking their references and talking with former clients, you should also ask them:

- Will you handle permits, or will I?
- Do you use subcontractors? If so, how do you hire them?
- Can you supply information on your license and insurance?
- How will you protect my property?
- What is the timeline for the project?

You should also discuss the payment structure. Different contractors take different approaches to project pricing. Some common structures include:

- **Guaranteed maximum prices:** This sets a maximum price for the project so you don't encounter any surprises. Before the project begins, the contractor shares a cost breakdown for it that you approve. If the project comes in under budget, you and the contractor will split the difference.
- **Lump sum:** With this approach, the contractor provides a lump-sum total price for the project without breaking down individual costs. You pay the lump sum, and if there is any excess, the contractor keeps the extra money.
- **Cost:** If a project is completed at cost, you pay for the cost of the project and the contractor's rate. If a project encounters delays or unexpected costs, you foot the bill.

What Types of Contractors Will You Need?

You'll need many different types of contractors during your lifetime as a landlord, from roofers to flooring contractors. Most commonly, though, you'll call on these four different types of contractors:

- **Lawn/snow:** This contractor will help maintain your property's lawn and landscaping as well as remove snow and help with winter prep. Choose landscape maintenance companies that can handle everything your property needs, including tree and shrub care, masonry repair, and outdoor lighting. That is, unless you just want a "mow and blow" service that does the bare minimum to keep the property attractive.
- **Electrician:** This contractor will complete tasks like running wiring and installing light switches.
- **Plumber:** This contractor will install pipes and connect drains to established piping systems.
- **Carpenter:** A carpenter will make your property stand out

by installing molding, creating built-ins, and handling other woodworking tasks.

BOOKKEEPING

You entered the real estate business to make money. Staying on top of your bookkeeping is crucial to understanding exactly how much you are making and spending in your business.

How Bookkeeping Works

Bookkeeping is essentially the recording of monetary transactions within a business. Typically, a bookkeeper will sit down weekly or monthly and record the business's transactions, including rent payments and property expenses. They'll also handle financial paperwork, like payroll, invoicing, or preparing financial statements for further analysis.

Why Bookkeeping Is Necessary

If you want a viable real estate business, you have to be able to make good financial decisions. Having up-to-date and balanced books helps you do that. The financial records a bookkeeper maintains can inform your decisions on your business's budget and help with tax preparation.

Do You Need to Hire a Bookkeeper?

Bookkeeping requires someone who is diligent, precise, and organized. You can handle bookkeeping duties yourself, delegate them to another employee, or hire a professional bookkeeper.

Whether you handle bookkeeping internally or outsource, decide on software to use or set up a spreadsheet to update regularly. Designate time to look over receipts and bank statements and update your books. Ideally, this should be completed weekly.

The key to keeping your books up to date is being organized and disciplined about recording transactions regularly. Be honest about whether you have the time to stay on top of this. If you don't, consider hiring someone to manage your bookkeeping for you. You won't regret outsourcing this task—having your books in order will help your business thrive and give you peace of mind that you're financially on the right track.

BUILD YOUR DOCUMENT LIBRARY

As a landlord, you'll find that there are some forms and paperwork you will use over and over again. Building a library of necessary forms and documents will help streamline property management and make it easier to grow your team in the future.

Some key forms you will need include:

- **Rental forms:** Have your rental application, welcome letters, and background check authorizations templated and ready to send.
- **Leases:** In addition to a basic lease agreement, you'll also want to have a month-to-month agreement, renewal agreement, addendums, and subleasing agreements ready to go.
- **Tenant notifications:** These forms can include disclosures, notices to enter, rental increase notices, maintenance updates, and eviction notices.
- **Violation notices:** Be prepared to inform tenants about past-due payments, smoking violations, pet violations, noise violations, damage, and other issues.

TAKEAWAYS

You didn't enter real estate investing to sit behind a desk managing tenants or handling repairs. By implementing the process I've outlined in this chapter and carefully growing your team, you'll be able to grow your business over time so you can be more hands-off. Trust me, there's nothing better than enjoying a drink with your partner or friends while your property manager handles the day-to-day operations of your business!

Takeaway #1: You're Only as Good as Your Tenant Screening Process

Tenants are the lifeblood of your business, and having good tenants who pay on time and respect the property as if it were their own is worth its weight in gold. Invest in designing a tenant screening process that thoroughly vets applicants. Track your procedures and processes so you can outsource these screening tasks when the time comes.

Takeaway #2: Don't Hesitate to Grow Your Team

You might not be in a position to grow your team right this moment. But one day, you will be ready. Have a plan for how you want to grow. Will you hire a property manager first, or outsource your bookkeeping? Develop a growth plan and create your processes with outsourcing in mind. It will be easier to seek help if you have a plan in place.

Takeaway #3: Always Be on the Lookout for Talent

The best time to search for a contractor or a property manager is when you don't need one. Keep a list of highly recommended tradesmen on hand and work to build relationships with them before you need assistance. After working together, don't hesitate to send them referrals or offer positive feedback. Relationships matter in this business.

WHAT'S NEXT

Your property management process is in place, and you have a plan to grow your team over time. Now, it's time to figure out exactly how to manage a short-term and mid-term rental so that your guests will return again and again.

In the next chapter, we'll cover how to set up each type of rental and what to expect from your guests. You'll be fully booked in no time at all!

FREE GIFT #2

The Complete Guide & Checklist to Tenant Screening: the secrets to getting dream tenants!

Finding and keeping good tenants can be a difficult endeavor but with the right steps you can avoid some of the headaches. This comprehensive guide will take you through the step-by-step process and best practices find the good ones. Learn how to attract ideal tenants, from conducting background and credit checks to verifying income and rental history. Avoid common mistakes and safeguard your investment with this essential tenant screening guide.

To access this free bonus, head to https://readstreetpress.com/rentalgift2 in your internet browser or scan the QR code below and I'll send it to you right away!

6

HOW TO MANAGE SHORT-TERM, MID-TERM, & VACATION RENTALS BETTER THAN THE RITZ CARLTON

"If you don't own a home, buy one. If you own a home, buy another one. If you own two homes, buy a third."

— JOHN PAULSON

Long-term rentals can provide a stable rental income. If you're in the right location, though, short-term, mid-term, and vacation rentals can be incredibly lucrative.

The key to making these types of rentals work is managing them effectively. A well-managed short-term, mid-term, or vacation rental can provide more upside for tenants than a hotel stay. For investors, these types of rentals can generate a lot of income in a short time frame because you can consistently bring in new tenants while increasing your prices.

In this chapter, I'm going to break down how you can turn a short-term, mid-term, or vacation rental into a cash cow.

SHORT-TERM/VACATION RENTALS

Demand for vacation rentals has outpaced hotels since 2022, according to an article from NerdWallet.

This shift makes sense. Short-term rentals offer perks like a kitchen, individual bedrooms, and backyards, making them a home away from home for travelers. They're the perfect option for digital nomads trying to work while they travel or large families who want to spend time together without splurging on multiple hotel rooms. While hotels offer some perks, they can't quite match the benefits of a vacation rental in the minds of many consumers. And it's not just budget-minded consumers. For example, a wealthy family planning a family reunion might be more amenable to renting a luxury home where everyone can be together and have privacy, rather than a busy hotel with shared common areas.

That's where you come in. With the right house in the right location, you can offer a vacation solution for travelers that far exceeds their hotel options.

Pros of Short-Term Rentals

There's a reason why short-term rentals are popping up in both established vacation destinations, like Nashville, and under-the-radar destinations, like Milwaukee. The benefits of owning a short-term rental are numerous, and real estate investors are trying to take advantage of this window of opportunity.

Here are some of the pros of owning a short-term rental:

More Cash

Short-term rentals can generate more cash per month than long-term rentals due to one simple factor: more tenants. For example, let's say you have a property within walking distance of the beach in a prominent vacation spot. You could charge $3,000 per month for a long-term rental. That's great money! But with a short-term rental, you can charge $2,500 per week. If you rent the property for four weeks a month, you collect $10,000. That's even better money!

Tax Benefits

Short-term rentals have a lot of expenses that can count as deductions, like cleaning fees, utilities, and insurance. These deductions can help you save money on your taxes. As always, work with a tax professional to fully understand the potential tax benefits of a short-term rental in your area.

More Control

Want to take a vacation at your rental? You can block out several weeks or months to live in your unit. Want to increase your income? You can raise prices for your next vacancy instead of waiting for a lease to expire. Want to perform some quick maintenance? When the current guests leave next weekend, you can knock out your tasks without anyone underfoot.

Cons of Short-Term Rentals

Do short-term rentals sound too good to be true? They can be a great investment, but they certainly aren't perfect.

Here are some cons to consider for short-term rentals:

Inconsistent Income

Yes, you can make more money on a short-term rental. However, you always have to be willing to accept that the income might be inconsistent based on seasonality and other factors. Have a plan for the months your unit sits vacant. That ski-in condo that's booked solid from November to April will sit vacant during "mud season" until the summer alpine activities draw more visitors. It will be vacant again in the fall after the foliage lovers have departed.

Increased Risk

Having an unpredictable income is a risk. If the economy tanks and people cut back on vacations, you could struggle. Your guests are also a risk. When you have more guests each month, the amount of time you have to vet them decreases. As a result, short-term rentals are more prone to theft or damage than long-term rentals. You can mitigate these risks to some extent by asking for a security deposit.

Area Limitations

Some areas are cracking down on short-term rentals. These restrictions might limit your ability to find a great property you can rent to vacationers. And, if you purchase a property and the restrictions change, you might have to sell the property much earlier than you intended. Check the local laws about short-term rentals in your area before you buy a property for that purpose.

How to Furnish a Short-Term Rental

Your guests can't bring their own furniture for a one-week stay in your beach house. You need to completely furnish a short-term rental so your guests can have a relaxing stay. These costs can add up quickly if you're not careful. Thankfully, there's a way to furnish your property without taking out a second mortgage.

What to Include

It might feel like you can furnish your short-term rental with left-over furniture from your college apartment, but I urge you not to take the easy way out. The way you furnish your rental impacts the amount you can charge and the overall satisfaction of your guests, which, in turn, influences your future earnings.

Before you create your shopping list, ask yourself the following questions:

- **Who is my ideal guest?** Will most of your guests be young women in town for a bachelorette party? Extended families enjoying a family reunion? Couples indulging in a romantic getaway? Each category requires different types of furnishing and amenities.
- **How big is the property?** The number of bedrooms and bathrooms will influence what you purchase. If you want to sleep more people than the bedrooms allow, you might want to add bunk beds, trundle beds, or a convertible sofa to your shopping list.
- **What is the property's vibe or aesthetic?** If your rental is a cabin in the woods, you might want to skip modern furnishings. Decide which look you are going for so you

can pick furniture and décor that creates an experience for your guests.

- **How much do I want to charge?** If you want to charge luxury prices, you need to spend a bit more on luxury furniture. If not, you might be able to save some money by finding durable pieces for a lower price.
- **What is my budget?** Do not go into debt furnishing your short-term rental. Examine your expenses and determine how much you can spend. Give yourself time to shop sales, and don't be afraid to reuse and recycle furniture as long as the pieces fit the vibe you are going for.

Once you know the profile of your ideal guest and the aesthetics you want to create, it's time to create your shopping list. Here are some recommendations to get you started:

- **Bedrooms:** At bare minimum, you'll need beds, nightstands, and a dresser. Think about how many people you want to sleep in each room. You might want a mix of king, queen, twin, and bunk beds to maximize your space.
- **Living areas:** You'll have couches, chairs, end tables, and, most likely, an entertainment system for the main living area of the house. Extras like a coffee table, dining table, and space for games and activities can also make the living area more inviting. A sleeper sofa can be an option if you cater to large families or groups.
- **Bathrooms:** Add a blow dryer, toiletries, and, if needed, extra storage to the bathroom to make it suitable for guests.
- **Kitchen:** Your guests will want dishes, cooking utensils, and a seating area so they can cook at home. Don't forget a coffee maker!
- **Backyard:** If you have an outdoor space, you might want to add some deck chairs, an outdoor dining table, or a grill so your guests can enjoy the space.

How to Estimate Costs

The cost to furnish your furniture can vary depending on your location and your shopping approach. To estimate costs, consider things like:

- **Your shopping style:** Are you a thrifting machine or do you prefer to buy new? Searching estate sales, thrift stores, and garage sales can help you save money and find some hidden gems.
- **Your location:** If you're in a remote area, you might need to ship items to your property, which can cost more. You might also need to rent a moving truck to transport furniture to the location.
- **Your timetable:** If you have several months to set up the property before guests arrive, you have more time to wait for sales or search for the perfect item. If you need to get the property ready quickly, you might need to snag items as soon as you find them.

After considering these factors, you can start to estimate your costs. If you ask ten short-term rental owners how much it cost to furnish their property, you'll get ten different answers. Let's do a sample estimate together.

For this estimate, let's pretend we're furnishing a four-bedroom, two-bathroom beach rental. The property is two blocks from the beach in a walkable beach town that's perfect for a family vacation. We want the property to be able to sleep ten people comfortably.

Here's the budget breakdown:

- **Bedrooms:** Two bedrooms will have queen beds, one will have a pair of twin beds, and the other will have two sets of bunk beds. We need to budget about $1,000-$2,000 for each bedroom.
- **Living room:** We want enough seating for ten people, a solid TV system, a coffee table for games, and plenty of lighting. This should cost about $2,000.

- **Kitchen/dining area:** We want a table that can seat ten people and a few bar stools for the island. This should cost $750 - $1,000.
- **Backyard:** The backyard is a huge selling point for this property. We want an outdoor dining area, nice chairs for the lawn, and a seating area for the porch. This adds $750-$1,000 to our budget.
- **Linens, toiletries, and utensils:** You'll need sheets for each bed, towels for each guest, and supplies for the kitchen. Plan to spend $2,000 - $2,500 on these items.
- **Appliances:** You want to offer a nice coffee maker in the kitchen, appliances like a toaster and blender, and hair dryers in the bathrooms. Set aside $750 for this category.

In this scenario, we live near the rental, so we'll transport most of the items ourselves. As you can see, all these expenses can add up really quickly. When you build your shopping list, do some research to determine the price range for each item and budget accordingly. If you find ways to save, take advantage of them!

Amenities

If you want to truly wow your guests—and earn great reviews that can help you charge premium prices—you'll want to have some amenities. The types of amenities you offer varies greatly based on your ideal guest's profile, location, and budget.

Some items to think about include:

- **Wi-Fi:** This is an amenity, but in reality, it's a necessity. Most guests expect super-quick Wi-Fi, so make sure you provide it. Multiple USB ports in the common areas and bedrooms are a nice perk, too.
- **Security:** Smart locks and Ring cameras can help you protect your property and make your guests feel safe.
- **Kitchen appliances:** A fully-stocked kitchen complete with a coffee bar and popular appliances will make it easier for guests to eat at the rental.
- **Extra toiletries:** Mini shampoo bottles, extra

toothbrushes, and other easy-to-forget items can save your guests a late-night run to the pharmacy.

- **Entertainment:** A deck of cards, board games, and paperback books can help your guests stay entertained during their downtime. You can also include items related to the location, like a boogie board or beach chairs for a beach rental or a sled and cozy blankets for a mountain rental.

Guest Books

Have you ever flipped through the guest book at a short-term rental? Whether you look through it at the beginning or the end of your stay, it probably left an impression on you about guests' overall experience at the rental.

A guest book can be a great opportunity for your guests to leave their best tips for future visitors and feedback for you. They can also help you collect more information on your guests so you can follow up with them later to see if they'd like to book another visit or build an email list for marketing.

Your guest book does not have to be complicated, either. A beautiful journal from a local shop and plenty of pens are more than enough to encourage your guests to leave a note.

Welcome Packets

Your visitors are in town for the vacation of a lifetime, but they're also guests in your home. A welcome packet helps you set expectations for their stay and gives instructions for check-out.

Feel free to get creative with your welcome packet, but always include these essential components:

- **Property information:** This is the place to let your guests know important info, like parking guidelines, Wi-Fi passwords, and how to contact you in case of an emergency.
- **Rules:** Let guests know any rules for the property, like noise guidelines and quiet hours.

- **Appliance guidelines:** Let them know which appliances are available and include instructions on how to use them.
- **Check-out instructions:** What do you need guests to do before you leave? Provide a checklist so they can prepare for their exit. Some popular tasks include stripping the beds, collecting towels for the laundry, or running a dishwasher cycle.

Your welcome packet is a living, breathing document. Don't be afraid to add pages and information to it as you receive feedback from your guests.

Guest Promotions and Local Suggestions

Your guests will be looking for fun things to do in the area, and this is your opportunity to be an excellent host. Consider what your guests might want to do locally and put together some recommendations to help them find local gems.

For instance, share your recommendations for:

- A local pizza place that will satisfy their hunger after a long day
- A vibey coffee shop that locals love
- A cute shop for gifts and souvenirs
- A nearby restaurant with photo-worthy views
- Kid-friendly activities the entire family can enjoy
- Breweries, wineries, or cocktail bars worth adding to a bar crawl

You can also partner with some of these businesses to offer guest promotions or discounts. Your guests will love saving a few dollars, the businesses will be grateful for the extra customers, and you'll build relationships with local venues that can pay off down the road.

Check-Out Instructions

You should include check-out instructions in your welcome packet so guests know what to expect. When putting together this document, it's important to be thorough and clear about your expectations.

Make sure these instructions include:

- **Check-out time:** Let guests know when they need to exit the property and any potential repercussions if they stay later than expected.
- **Lock-up information:** Tell guests where to leave their keys and remind them to lock every door when they leave.
- **Cleaning instructions:** Let guests know where to place dirty towels and linens, how to dispose of trash, and any other expectations for cleaning the home before they depart.
- **Lights and utilities:** Remind guests to turn off all lights and let them know the desired temperature for the thermostat.

How to Price Your Short-Term Rental

Ready to make some money? If you want to maximize your profit, you need to price your short-term rental appropriately for your goals and location. You need to ask yourself several questions before setting your rental price. I'm going to break them down one by one.

How Much Will It Take to Operate?

Just like a long-term rental, it takes money to operate a short-term rental. Write down the cost of your monthly mortgage, expected utility payments, insurance, listing fees, and additional fees for cleaning services and a property manager, if you have one.

What Extras Do I Want to Provide?

If you want to provide extras like cable or satellite TV, a welcome basket filled with local goods, or amenities like bicycles or kayaks, add them to your operating expenses. You don't want these items to come out of your pocket, so calculate how much you spend on these items per visit and roll them into your price.

What Should My Nightly Rate Be?

After you calculate your operating expenses, it's time to calculate your nightly rate. The average month is 30 days, so divide your expenses by 30. This will give you the bare minimum you should charge per night.

Of course, your goal is to make a profit, not just cover your expenses. Think about how much you might need over the course of the year for repairs and maintenance, as well as your desired profit, and add that to the bare minimum nightly rate.

What Are the Service Fees?

You will need to clean the property after every visit. You might also want to allow pets, in which case you will likely charge a pet fee. If you list through a platform like Airbnb or Vrbo, you might also have to consider listing fees. Decide what you will charge for each of these services and outline them for your guests.

What Is My Expected Vacancy Rate?

Chances are, your property will not be booked for every night it's available. For example, if your property is located in an area that is great for weekend visits, you might not have the property booked during the week. If your property is a cabin in a popular ski area, you might not be booked during "mud season." Think about how often you expect your property to book, and be realistic about the location and potential seasonal ebbs and flows.

If you expect your property to be vacant for days or months at a time, you need to consider how you will cover expenses like your mortgage, HOA fees, landscape maintenance, and utilities. In some cases, you may want to increase your rental price during busy times to offset the losses later on.

After you've answered these questions, it's time to experiment with your prices. Set aside some time with your calculator and play around with potential rates. Look at other rentals in your area to determine what other property owners charge for comparable properties. Be prepared to adjust your prices as the market changes and as you rack up positive reviews about the property.

How to Set Up an Airbnb Listing

Airbnb changed the game for short-term rentals, and you'll have to list your rental on the platform if you want to find renters, especially in the beginning. Consider this section your crash course on the platform.

How to List on Airbnb

Depending on your location and property type, you will likely face a lot of competition with other rentals for bookings. Your listing can help set you apart and shoot you to the top of the search results—if you have the right approach.

- **Conduct SEO research:** Think of Airbnb as the Google for short-term rentals. You need to know what your ideal renter is looking for so you can include those terms in your description. Enter various keywords into Airbnb and see what pops up. How do popular properties describe their rental?
- **Write a good description:** The more information you can include in your description, the better. Include the information you gathered from your research and be as descriptive as possible. What amenities do you offer? How close is your property to desirable entertainment? Great photos will get your property rented fast, even more so than a description. We've included some photo tips below.
- **Set competitive prices:** Know the average price for rentals in your area and set your prices accordingly. Understand how your rental compares to listings at the highest price point in your area and the lowest.
- **Consider outsourcing:** Yes, there are people who write rental listings for a living. These professionals are experts in optimizing your listing for each platform, so consider investing in their services to get a leg up on the competition.

What to Know About Fees

Airbnb is a business, not a charity. As a host, Airbnb helps you by marketing your property to guests through their advertising and name recognition. It also offers protections, customer support, and resources to help you run a profitable business. As a result, it charges fees.

The fees Airbnb charges fluctuate based on the property location and cancellation policies. You have two options when it comes to paying these fees: you can cover all the costs as the host, or you can split the fee with your guests.

In some cases, you will be required to use the host-only option, also called the Simplified Pricing option. Simplified Pricing applies if you are a software-connected host, which means you use some sort of software to manage your property. As of 2024, hosts paid 15% to Airbnb using the Simplified Pricing structure. However, guests see that the service fee is $0. This lack of service fee can often lead to a higher booking rate because it benefits guests compared to splitting the fee.

With split-fee pricing, the host pays about 3% of the Airbnb fees, and the guest pays anywhere from 13%-20%. This structure helps offset your costs, but can be a deterrent for guests wanting to book your property.

If you have the option to use split-fee or Simplified Pricing, play around with different rates to determine how much you will profit from either option. Pick the option that is right for you.

What to Include in Your Listing Photos

You can include up to 100 photos in your Airbnb listing, but don't let that overwhelm you. A handful of incredible photos will have a bigger impact on your booking rate than 100 subpar photos.

You can hire someone to take photos of your listing. If you prefer doing it yourself, implement these tips to make them stand out:

- **Keep the unit clutter-free:** Make sure surfaces are clear and there are no papers on the countertops or other areas.

- **Make sure it's clean:** Take photos after thoroughly cleaning the property.
- **Spotlight amenities:** Add a photo of the stocked coffee bar or the board game collection to let guests know about the perks your property offers.
- **Work your angles:** Shoot from the corner to capture the entire space, or take a photo looking down at the open living space from the second floor.
- **Make sure it's well-lit:** Use natural lighting to depict the brightness of the rooms or turn on lamps in the bedroom to give it a cozy vibe.
- **Add photos of local attractions and amenities:** These photos may include a quaint downtown street, a sandy beach, a boat dock, ski slopes, hiking trails, lakes, etc.

What to Know About Reviews

Reviews will make or break your success as a short-term rental owner. You want your guests to leave great reviews after every stay because reviews increase your visibility in Airbnb's search results and encourage future guests to book your property.

Ultimately, you can't control if guests leave a review or not, but you can do a few things to encourage them. My favorite ways to encourage reviews include:

- **Making the request at check-out:** Add it to your check-out checklist to remind guests to leave feedback.
- **Posting signage around the property:** Type up a one-sheet asking guests to leave a review. Frame it and display it near your guestbook or welcome packet.
- **Reviewing the guests:** Airbnb offers double-blind reviews, which allow you to review your guests after every stay. When you review a guest, they receive a notification reminding them to review you as well.

How to Become a Superhost

Airbnb is a crowded platform, so you need to stand out to secure listings. The Superhost badge is one way to do this, but it takes some time to achieve.

When you become a Superhost, Airbnb adds a badge to your profile indicating your status. The badge helps potential guests identify hosts who offer great properties. Approximately 20% of hosts earn Superhost status, according to AirDNA.

To become a Superhost, you need to:

- Maintain a 4.8 overall rating.
- Maintain a cancellation rate of under 1%, with the exception of cancellations that meet requirements for extenuating circumstances.
- Have a 90% response rate or above.
- Complete ten trips or three reservations that total 100 nights of occupancy.

See? It's not easy to reach this status. Airbnb evaluates hosts quarterly and hands out Superhost badges automatically based on the above criteria. If you land the coveted badge, there are some benefits, including:

- **Additional promotion:** Airbnb includes Superhost properties on promotional materials and offers a search filter for travelers so they can separate Superhosts from other listings
- **Referral bonus:** You can receive 20% more than the standard bonus for hosts you refer to the platform.
- **Extra coupons:** If you maintain Superhost status for a year, you receive a $100 coupon.
- **Priority service:** Customer support will prioritize your needs if issues arise.
- **Early access:** You'll have access to new features before anyone else.

In addition, you might see an increase in bookings. The Superhost badge can build trust with potential guests, which can set you apart from other properties in your area.

How to Manage a Short-Term Rental

Just like long-term rentals, short-term rentals require hands-on management. From maintaining listings to handling repairs, there are plenty of day-to-day responsibilities that need to be handled to own a successful short-term rental.

Most real estate investors use one of four options to manage their property rentals. The right option for you will depend on your budget and goals for your real estate venture.

Self

Yes, you can manage your short-term rental yourself. This approach saves you money but costs you time. To manage your short-term rental effectively, you will need to:

- **Price your rental:** You will need to set prices for your property, keep up to date with the rental market in your area, and adjust prices accordingly.
- **Manage the money:** You will have to keep your books balanced and manage income and expenses to make sure your property is actually generating a profit.
- **Market the property:** From coordinating listing photos to updating property descriptions, you will need to market your property properly.
- **Protect your property:** You want your property to stay safe, which means enforcing house rules and screening guests.
- **Maintain the property:** This entails managing the cleaning service and scheduling or performing maintenance.
- **Handle customer service:** If the barbeque grill doesn't have gas or the air conditioning breaks, guests will call you for help.

Property Manager

You can outsource all the aforementioned tasks to a property manager. A property manager allows you to be hands-off. They handle the listings, bookings, and inquiries (and can list the property on multiple platforms). Once the guests arrive, the property manager will provide customer service, handle logistics such as linens and toiletries, and take care of cleaning the property after guests check out.

Some managers charge a commission, meaning they charge 25%-40% of the rental income. Others work on a fixed-price basis, meaning you pay them a set fee every month. Shop around for a property manager who performs the services you need for your rental at a price you can afford. Some states require that a property manager be licensed. Property managers are full-service and charge accordingly. For a cheaper option, consider a co-host.

Co-Hosting

You can also hire someone to co-host your property on Airbnb. Co-hosting means you hire someone to help you manage the property, especially the guest experience. Co-hosting benefits owners who don't have the time to manage a listing once guests arrive. You can find co-hosts in your area or through marketplaces like CohostClub. Typically, a co-host charges 20%-25% of the rental fee or a fixed price rate. Unlike property managers, co-hosts do not handle the bookings; their role is simply to ensure an outstanding guest experience.

Virtual Assistance

You also don't have to delegate every aspect of property management. You can hire a virtual assistant to take certain tasks off your plate. There are virtual assistants who have extensive experience assisting real estate investors. They can perform tasks like responding to guest inquiries, managing your listing, and coordinating cleaning and maintenance.

Other Short-Term Rental Platforms

Airbnb is a great way to market your short-term rental, but it's not your only option. Explore other platforms like:

- Vrbo
- PlumGuide
- FlipKey

Every short-term rental platform has its own unique criteria and client base. Research the right ones for you based on your location, property type, and cost. You might find a platform that generates more bookings than Airbnb!

MID-TERM RENTALS

A mid-term rental is a happy medium between vacation rentals and long-term leases. With the right location and target tenant, it can be incredibly lucrative.

Pros of Mid-Term Rentals

Mid-term rentals provide housing to a typically under-served portion of the rental marketplace: people in a time of transition. Some of the pros of mid-term rentals include:

Longer Lease Terms

Mid-term leases typically last 3 to 9 months, making them the middle ground for people who aren't looking for a short stay, but can't commit to a long-term lease. As a landlord, you receive the benefits of a steady income while still being able to bring in new tenants and periodically raise prices.

Good Tenants

Most people seek mid-term rentals because they want the comforts of home for a short time frame. Your tenants will typically be traveling nurses, digital nomads, professionals working a consulting or other limited gig, students, or families who are relocating.

More Stable

The short-term rental market can change with the seasons—and the weather. Vacationers might cancel their trip due to impending weather, financial issues, or family emergencies. Tenants in mid-term leases are using your property as their residence, so they're less likely to change a booking at the last minute.

Cons of Mid-Term Rentals

There are some challenges associated with mid-term rentals. Some of the cons include:

Less Potential Income

Mid-term rentals will typically generate less income than short-term rentals because you are housing one tenant at a time for a locked-in price. You'll also need to consider the price your tenant can afford to pay in rent. A student might be able to afford less than, say, a traveling nurse.

Higher Turnover

We've talked about the cost of preparing a property for new tenants several times throughout this book. Mid-term rentals face more turnover than long-term rentals, albeit less than short-term rentals.

Increased Upfront Costs

Unlike long-term rentals, mid-term rentals need to be furnished. You'll have to fund furnishing the home, just like a short-term rental, without the benefit of premium rental prices.

How Mid-Term Rentals Compare to Short-Term Rentals

There is a lot of overlap between mid-term and short-term rentals. Both types of rentals need to be furnished, although you can likely reduce the amenities offered for a mid-term rental.

When it comes to pricing, both mid-term and short-term rentals will likely generate more income than a long-term rental. On paper, a short-term rental could generate the highest return—but you would need to keep it fully booked, which is hard to guarantee. A mid-term rental might generate less income per month, but you might see fewer vacancies, depending on the location and your target tenant.

A Hidden Moneymaker: Traveling Nurses

If your property is near a hospital, you might be sitting on a gold mine. Hospitals regularly employ traveling nurses who take on new assignments in new cities every few months. They need stable housing, but don't want to lock themselves into a year-long lease.

This group needs a fully furnished rental, but they aren't looking for extras like toiletries. They also tend to prefer 3 to 9-month leases.

If you want to reach these renters, list your property on Airbnb, Vrbo, or FurnishedFinder. You can also let your local hospital's recruiting department know that you have housing available for their new hires.

Corporate and Business Rentals

If you have several local corporations or large businesses in your area, you might be able to fill your mid-term rental with people relocating for a job or consultants on months-long projects.

Searching for permanent housing can be stressful. If you have a property in a good school district and desirable location, it can be a good option for families who are relocating due to new employment or a transfer. A mid-term rental is ideal because it provides permanent housing for a short time while they look for their dream home and explore the area.

TAKEAWAYS

The real estate space is filled with gurus promising quick returns on short-term and mid-term rentals. They can be lucrative, but they can also be challenging. Consider everything I've laid out in this chapter before deciding what type of rental you want to offer. Once you've made your decision, do everything you can to make your rental the most desirable on the market!

Takeaway #1: Consider Your Location and Target Renter

Your location and target renter will influence a lot of your decision-making as a real estate investor. A short-term rental might not work in a college town, while a mid-term rental might not be the best choice for a beach haven. Let the market drive your decision, not your emotions.

Takeaway #2: Understand the Costs

There are more costs associated with a short or mid-term rental, especially upfront. You'll need to furnish the property and provide amenities. There's also a time cost, too. If you plan to manage the property yourself, be prepared to spend more time marketing and maintaining the rental.

Takeaway #3: Set the Right Price

Do plenty of market research before setting your price and experiment with potential rates to find the sweet spot for your property. Understand that seasonality can impact the price you can charge at different parts of the year, and make sure you charge enough during busy times to offset vacancies.

WHAT'S NEXT

You've learned everything you need to know about purchasing and renting your first property. In the next chapter, we'll dream big. I'll teach you how to grow your portfolio so you can become a real estate mogul.

FREE GIFT #3

The Only Maintenance Checklist for Rental Properties You'll Ever Need: don't let anything fall through the cracks!

Repairs and maintenance on your investment is unavoidable but does not have to be overbearing. With this maintenance checklist you will learn how to upkeep your property, prevent small issues from becoming major problems, keep your tenants happy and maintain your property value.

To access this free bonus, head to https://readstreetpress.com/rentalgift3 in your internet browser or scan the QR code below and I'll send it to you right away!

7

HOW TO BECOME A REAL ESTATE MOGUL BIGGER THAN ROBERT KIYOSAKI

"Often in the real world, it's not the smart who get ahead, but the bold."

— *ROBERT KIYOSAKI*

That Robert Kiyosaki quote above? It fires me up, especially as I grow as a real estate investor.

There will always be someone who is technically smarter than you. But bolder than you? That's entirely in your control.

You took a bold step when you picked up this book. The rest of your real estate journey will also be built on bold steps as you scale your portfolio, learn to manage multiple properties, and grow your network with other people who can help with your journey.

In this chapter, I'm going to break down each of those bold steps individually. By the end of it, you'll be well on your way to becoming a true real estate mogul.

HOW TO SCALE A BULLETPROOF PORTFOLIO

Earlier in this book, you learned how to find excellent properties and finance their purchase. Any real estate investor can find a solid property once and turn a profit. But to do it over and over again takes a combination of skill, creativity, and capital.

Create a Growth Plan

Yes, you want to be bold as you scale. That doesn't mean you need to be foolish. You wouldn't take a road trip without bringing a map. On the same principle, you don't build a profitable real estate business flying by the seat of your pants.

Review the strategy you developed in chapter 2. What did you target for your first property? Consider finding a similar property for your second purchase. This approach allows you to build on what you already know, and, hopefully, find, purchase, and list your next property quickly.

However, you will eventually want to diversify. Include this timeline in your growth plan. For example, if your first property was a long-term residential rental, you might want to move into the commercial space.

Revisit this plan regularly to make sure you are on track and adjust as needed.

Find and Leverage More Capital

Once your first rental property starts generating income, it can be tempting to sock the cash into your personal bank account. Don't do it. To build a real estate business that can truly free you from your 9-to-5, you need more properties.

Instead, use that money and, if needed, some of the financing options we discussed in chapter 4 to purchase the types of properties you identified in your growth plan. Once you've purchased your second property, use that income to fund your third. Rinse, repeat, get rich.

Search for More Value

When you purchased your first property, you might've had very little to put down for a down payment or had a poor credit score that limited your financing options. Hopefully, you will be in a better position for your next purchase.

Review your financial standing again. Can you contribute more for a down payment this time around, thus lowering your mortgage payment and increasing your rental profit? Can you look forward to better loan terms due to better credit?

You might also be able to search for more value within the property you buy. For example, you might be able to use the rental income from your first property to make more improvements in the second property that can increase its rental value. Be creative as you search for more value in the properties you plan to purchase and the properties you already have in your portfolio.

Expand and Adapt

As you look toward the future, consider expanding into new markets. For example, if you've already purchased a rental property in your current city, consider adding a short-term rental in your favorite vacation destination to give you access to a whole new market.

Above all, keep learning. Be a constant student of real estate. Read more books like this, sign up for email newsletters to receive the latest updates about the industry, and pursue every opportunity to learn from real estate moguls a few steps ahead of you.

MANAGING MULTIPLE PROPERTIES

We talked a lot about how to manage a property in chapter 5. As your portfolio grows, you'll need those tips more than ever. Here's what you can do as you scale to manage multiple properties without losing your mind.

Get Organized

Simple? Yes. The difference between success and failure as a real estate professional? Absolutely. Think about everything you need to keep track of for your first rental: receipts, contracts, rental agreements, forms, and more. In addition to the paperwork, you also need to pay taxes, balance your books, and field inquiries from potential new tenants.

It's a lot of work. Now multiply that by 3, 5, or 10 properties. It would be unmanageable. That's why you need to be organized. Develop a system to remind you about important deadlines and other dates. Create a filing system for digital and paper files so you always have them on hand. Whatever you create, make sure it is something you can teach to a new hire.

Build a Team

It is possible to manage your first few properties by yourself. But you only have so much time and energy, so you'll eventually need to hire team members as you scale. For example, you might decide to hire a bookkeeper after purchasing your second property, or a property manager after purchasing your third.

Trust me, you will expand your team eventually. This is why it's helpful to be organized and build scalable systems for rental applications, bookkeeping, and other tasks from the beginning. When you hand the reins over to your new employee, they'll be ready to jump right in and pick up where you left off.

Utilize Software

It's pretty great living in the future. We can ask Alexa to turn on the lights, set the thermostat from our phone, and talk into our Apple watches to respond to text messages. Technology certainly makes everyday life easier—and it can make managing your rentals easier, too.

Consider implementing software programs to streamline key portfolio management tasks. Some popular options include:

- AppFolio Investment Manager
- SyndicationPro
- DoorLoop

Research your options and ask your network for recommendations.

GROWING YOUR NETWORK AND DOING BIGGER DEALS

You can hardly believe it. The chance to purchase a 15-unit apartment building in a prime location in your growing city just came across your desk. The only problem? You have nowhere near the capital to invest in a property like that on your own, no matter how much money you make.

To complete a big deal like that, you'll need a partner. The best time to start looking for a real estate partner is before you need one.

How to Network

Real estate investing is all about relationships. Yes, you might compete with other investors on a deal or two. But having friends in the industry, from new investors like yourself to established veterans with a phone-book-sized portfolio, can help your business grow in ways you can never imagine.

Start networking as early as possible by:

- Attending local real estate events
- Traveling to national real estate conferences
- Joining professional associations like the National Real Estate Investors Association
- Cultivating relationships with everyone you meet

Networking can be intimidating, especially when you are first starting out. Keep pushing! You'll find some friends and mentors who provide encouragement and knowledge.

How to Complete Bigger Deals

If you want to participate in bigger deals like the apartment scenario I outlined above, you might need a partner. There are typically two types of partnerships: active partnerships and passive income partnerships. In an active partnership, you and your partners share operations tasks equally. In a passive partnership, you raise money from investors who won't be as involved in the operations.

Partnerships are a great way to combine your resources and lean on the expertise of more experienced investors. However, you'll be splitting the earnings and will have to compromise as you purchase and manage the property.

Your network will be a great resource for potential partners. You could also search for investing partners online or through crowd-funding platforms.

TAKEAWAYS

You picked up this book because you had big dreams about investing in real estate. You're well on your way to making them happen. Scaling your portfolio, managing multiple properties, and taking on bigger deals will take some bold steps. You can make them happen by implementing the steps I outlined above.

Takeaway #1: Start Right Now

If you have just one rental property right now, you have the gift of time. You have time to develop a plan to diversify your portfolio. You have time to get organized and create systems to use in your business as you purchase new properties. You have time to grow your network and prepare for partnerships. Take advantage of this additional time and use it to set your business up for success.

Takeaway #2: Keep Learning

It can be intimidating to learn real estate management software. It can be scary to walk into a networking event when you don't know anyone. It can be downright terrifying to purchase another property when you're still learning how to manage one. Remember that every scary step is a chance to grow your knowl-edge. But as they say, "Fortune favors the bold." Every expert was once a beginner. Ask the questions, do the research, and pursue relationships. Above all, keep learning.

Takeaway #3: Don't Stay Stuck

Making bold moves means you might make some missteps. That's okay! The worst thing you can do as a real estate investor is stay stagnant. Pursue diverse types of properties, explore new markets, and pursue bigger deals.

WHAT'S NEXT

In this chapter, you prepared to acquire new properties and scale your business. Daydreaming about your business's growth is a lot of fun, but it's also important to think about the end game for every property you purchase. In the next chapter, we'll talk about potential exit strategies.

FREE GIFT #4

The Ultimate Tax Planning E-Book for Real Estate Investors: don't miss out on any deductions!

Learn about the various deductions and tax benefits available in this e-book. From depreciation and mortgage interest, this book will help you catch potential tax savings. Keep more of your hard-earned money! Ask your CPA for more information about the potential deductions your real estate portfolio can create for you.

To access this free e-book, head to https://readstreetpress.com/rentalgift4 in your internet browser or scan the QR code below and I'll send it to you right away!

8

THE MUST-KNOW EXIT STRATEGIES TO PROTECT YOUR EMPIRE

"Every exit is an entry somewhere else."

— *TOM STOPPARD*

When you're handed the keys to your first rental property, the last thing you're thinking about is your exit strategy. This oversight is a mistake.

Whenever you invest in something, whether a real estate property or a stock, you should have an exit strategy in place when you make your purchase. An exit strategy is essentially a contingency plan. It is your plan for how you will liquidate an asset once you've met or exceeded a specific set of criteria.

In real estate investing, there are several exit strategies you can use. In this chapter, I'll review each one so you can make the best decision for your business with each investment you make.

HOLD FOREVER

This exit strategy is exactly as it sounds. When you purchase a property with a "hold forever" exit strategy, it means you plan to hang on to it for the rest of your life. In many cases, you might pass it on to your heirs when you die. This strategy allows you to build equity in the property, collect rent, and upgrade the rental to increase its overall value.

Investors tend to choose this strategy to generate recurring income and hedge against inflation. It also offers some tax benefits, like owner expense deductions.

The downfall of this strategy centers on the real estate cycle. As we discussed in chapter 1, the real estate market ebbs and flows. Changes in the local, state, and national real estate market can impact the home's monthly rental prices. If you plan to hold on to the property long-term to generate recurring income, be prepared for those prices to fluctuate.

SELL AND CASH OUT

This exit strategy is the most popular for real estate investors. In this scenario, you plan to eventually sell the property for a profit. This sale could take place immediately after a little rehabbing or a decade from now after collecting rent.

This exit strategy has similar benefits and drawbacks to a hold forever strategy. The only difference is that you envision selling at some point, usually when the market reaches its peak.

SELLER FINANCING

In chapter 4, we discussed seller financing options. Remember, seller financing is a way to purchase a home without using a traditional lender. When you use this as an exit strategy for your property, you are in the seller's position instead of the buyer's. This approach allows you to collect monthly payments, spread out your tax burden, and sell the property at the end of the deal.

However, this approach can be risky. Since your buyer is responsible for the monthly payments, but you still hold the title, any default will impact you. If the buyer can't pay, you could enter foreclosure.

1031 EXCHANGE

Capital gains taxes can be pricey. A 1031 Exchange is a popular strategy investors use to minimize their tax burden. With a 1031 Exchange, you essentially swap one property for another and defer taxes in the process. For example, if you profit $15,000 from the sale of your first rental property, you can use the proceeds on your next property. When you do this, you don't defer paying capital gains taxes, which is typically 15%-20% of the sale.

This approach is a great way to consolidate your properties as your business grows or increase your ROI for your money by upgrading your portfolio.

As you can imagine, this type of exchange is complicated. Make sure you work with a tax professional to execute it properly and avoid additional scrutiny from the IRS.

TAKEAWAYS

Many new real estate investors purchase properties without an exit strategy in mind, and it gets them into trouble down the road. Consider each of the strategies outlined in this chapter carefully and enter into each purchase with your exit in mind. It will make it much easier to decide whether to exit the property when the time comes.

Takeaway #1: Consider the Market

Revisit the real estate cycle as you decide your exit strategy, especially if you plan to sell and cash out. Consider how long it will take to get the desired ROI on your investment based on the phase the local, state, and national real estate market is in. Make sure you can financially handle keeping the property longer than planned.

Takeaway #2: Seek Assistance

Exit strategies like 1031 Exchanges or seller financing can be difficult to execute on your own. Seek help from an attorney to help you create contracts to use with your buyer for a seller financing agreement. Use a tax professional to assist with a 1031 Exchange.

Takeaway #3: It's Okay to Change Your Mind

Yes, you might've bought a property intending to hold it forever and pass it down to whoever inherits or buys your business in the future. But things change. Don't be afraid to pivot your exit strategy if your circumstances—or the market—dictate it. Your exit strategy should be written in pencil, not permanent ink.

WHAT'S NEXT

Whew! This chapter might've been short and sweet, but we've covered a lot of ground throughout this book. We'll wrap everything up in the pages to come.

FREE GIFT #5

Free Chapter From Our Upcoming Book: *The Complete LLC Beginners Guide: The Easy Way to Create & Manage Your Limited Liability Company, Save on Taxes & Avoid Costly Mistakes*

Creating an LLC is an essential part of running your real estate portfolio and protecting yourself. Get a sneak peek into our upcoming book with this free chapter on creating and managing your LLC. Learn the easy steps needed to establish your LLC and take advantage of tax benefits. Whether you're just beginning or looking to optimize your existing business, this chapter will give you the place to start your path to success.

To access this free chapter, head to https://readstreetpress.com/rentalgift5 in your internet browser or scan the QR code below and I'll send it to you right away!

CONCLUSION

"When one door closes, buy another one and open it yourself."

— ANONYMOUS

Sometimes, I think about who I was before starting my real estate journey. That version of myself feels like a completely different person, so much so that I still call him Old Andrew in my mind.

Old Andrew was miserable. He was bored. He had so many dreams and so little time to actually chase them.

I like New Andrew—the version writing this to you right now—so much better. Now, I don't think about commuting to the office; I think about the next plane I'm hopping on with my wife. I don't think about packing a soggy sandwich to eat at my desk; I think about the next gourmet meal I'm going to whip up for friends and family. I don't sit up at night, worrying about my next annual review with the boss; instead, I dream about the DIY projects I'm going to tackle around the house.

Real estate investing made that type of financial and time freedom happen for me. Now that you've read this book, it can happen for you, too.

WHAT TO REMEMBER

We covered a lot in this book. If you're feeling a little overwhelmed right now, don't worry. You're not alone—I felt overwhelmed a lot when I started my real estate investing journey. It's why I wrote this book!

I hope you refer back to this book often as you pursue your first deal, welcome your first tenants, and grow your business. In the meantime, remember these key takeaways:

- **Don't skip the strategy:** You need a strategy for purchasing a property, financing a property, and growing your business.
- **Real estate investing is not one-size-fits-all:** Think creatively about searching for properties and financing your deals, and think about how much risk you're willing and able to take on.
- **Know your market:** Do your research and make decisions based on data, not feelings. Study your market and keep learning.
- **Just start:** This book is your blueprint for launching and growing your business. It's useless if it just sits on your shelf or on your Kindle.

This book exists because I know anyone can find success in real estate investing. You just need the right strategy and the knowledge to make it happen. There's room for all of us in this industry. Use this book to build the business of your dreams.

YOUR NEW LIFE IS JUST AROUND THE CORNER

Before we end our time together, I want you to grab a piece of paper. On one side, describe the current version of yourself. How do you feel? How do you spend your time? What are your dreams?

Then, I want you to turn the paper over and picture the new version of yourself. How does that version of you spend time?

What are your hobbies and dreams? What are your relationships like?

It is possible to be that new version of yourself. I'm living proof of it. And I want that for you—it's why I wrote this book. Now, it's time to snag your first real estate deal and start your journey. I'm rooting for you!

To your success,

Andrew

THANK YOU

THANK YOU so much for buy and reading my book! You could have picked from many others, but you chose this one.

Before you go, I want to ask you for one small favor.

Can you please leave this book a review on Amazon?

Leaving a review is the best way to support the work of independent authors like me. You can scan the QR code or visit the link below:

https://www.amazon.com/review/create-review/?asin= B0D3R8SZRQ

Your feedback will help me to keep writing the kind of books that will help you build the real estate empire of your dreams. It would mean a lot to me to hear from you.

PERMANENT PTO

Spend Life Living

Our mission is to inspire and empower others to break free from the constraints of traditional employment and achieve Permanent PTO through entrepreneurship. We believe everyone can transform their financial future and live the life they've always dreamed of and spend life living.

If you would like more resources, please visit our website: www.permanentpto.com

WOULD YOU LIKE MORE OF OUR BOOKS FOR FREE?

Join Our Exclusive ARC Team—Limited Spots Available!

Do you love being the first to discover groundbreaking books? If so, you're invited to apply for our Advanced Review Copy (ARC) Team!

As a member of this elite group, you'll receive early copies of our upcoming books—completely free. All we ask in return is your honest feedback so we can improve the quality of our content. This is your chance to get exclusive access, influence the book market, and connect with authors and fellow readers.

Why Apply?

• **Early Access:** Be among the first to read and review new titles before they hit the shelves.

• **Influence Others:** Your insights help guide other readers and shape future publications.

• **Exclusive Content:** Get free access to new articles, tools, and more!

Spots are limited to ensure a quality experience for all members. Don't miss this opportunity to make a real impact in the world of real estate and entrepreneurship literature.

Apply online with the QR code or visit https://readstreetpress.com/freebooks to join our ARC Reviewers Team. We look forward to having you!

GLOSSARY

Annualized ROI: A property's ROI divided by the number of years you expect to hold the property.

Assumable mortgage: A type of financing in which a buyer takes over a seller's existing mortgage.

Average annual return: The sum of the expected ROI for every year you plan to hold the property divided by the number of years you expect to hold the property.

Buy box: A list of criteria for the property you plan to purchase.

Buy, rehab, rent, refinance, repeat (BRRR): A real estate strategy that involves purchasing a property, renovating it, leasing it, refinancing it, and snowballing the cash into another property purchase.

C-corporation (C-corp): An entity in which the business owners are taxed personally rather than as a business.

Capital expenses: The amount of potential expenditures, like home improvements or maintenance.

Capitalization rate: The net operating income divided by the purchase price of the property.

Cash-on-cash return: The property's annual cash flow divided by the amount of money invested in the property.

Cash flow: The amount of money entering and leaving the business.

Cash flow after taxes: The amount of money left after subtracting taxes from gross revenue.

Cash flow before taxes: Your net operating income minus debt service and capital expenses, plus loan additions.

Cash for keys: An exchange in which a landlord pays a tenant an agreed-upon fee to exit the property.

Conventional loan: A mortgage, typically with 15-year to 30-year payment terms.

Cure or quit notice: A notice used during the eviction process if a tenant is in violation of the lease.

Debt service: The amount you will pay on your mortgage annually.

Due diligence: The process in which a buyer researches a property, including a title inspection, document inspection, and physical inspection.

Earnest money deposit: A sum of money, typically 1%-3% of the price of the home, provided in good faith to show the seller a buyer is serious about their offer.

Eviction: The process of removing a tenant from a property due to a violation.

Forced appreciation: An increase in a property's value due to the investor's decisions, like renovations or other property improvements.

Gross operating income: All the income you expect your property to generate annually.

Holding mortgage: An agreement in which the seller provides a loan and keeps the property title until the buyer pays for the property in full.

Home equity line of credit (HELOC): A line of credit that allows someone to borrow against the equity in their home.

House hacking: Renting out part of your home to other tenants and using the income to cover your mortgage or additional expenses.

Internal rate of return: An estimate of how much the property will earn while you own it.

Limited liability company (LLC): A type of business entity that separates the business from the business owner to protect the owner's assets.

Loan additions: The amount of money paid annually for a non-mortgage loan.

Long-term rentals: Rentals with lease terms of 12 months or more.

Mid-term rentals: Rentals with lease terms of several months.

Multifamily property: A property that can house multiple families at once, like an apartment building or condominium complex.

Natural appreciation: An increase in a property's value due to market forces outside the investor's control, like the economy.

Negative cash flow: The state of cash flow when expenses exceed income.

Net operating income: Gross operating income minus operating expenses.

Operating expenses: The amount of money needed to maintain the property, pay taxes, and advertise vacancies.

Pay or quit notice: A notice used during the eviction process if a tenant owes unpaid rent.

Portfolio loan: A loan in which the lender finances, keeps, and services the loan in their own portfolio.

Positive cash flow: The state of cash flow when income exceeds expenses.

Rent-to-own agreement: A type of seller financing in which a renter pays the seller an option fee that enables them to purchase the property later.

Residential property: A home inhabited by the owner or tenants.

Return on investment (ROI): A percentage that helps determine how much profit your investment will generate.

S-corporation (S-corp): A pass-through entity that shifts income and liabilities to shareholders.

Seller financing: A type of financing in which a seller pays the property owner for the property instead of the bank.

Short-term rentals: These rentals are typically vacation properties.

Single-family residential: A property occupied by one family.

Unconditional quit notice: A notice used during the eviction process if a tenant needs to vacate immediately due to illegal activity or gross negligence.

REFERENCES

2023 Home Buyers and Sellers Generational Trends Report. (2023). National Association of Realtors Research Group. https://cdn.nar.realtor/sites/default/files/documents/2023-home-buyers-and-sellers-generational-trends-report-03-28-2023.pdf?_gl= 1*1yzyzs*_gcl_au*MjAwNzcwNDMwNi4xNjg3MjgwMTI4

4 Valid Reasons a Landlord Can Evict a Tenant. (2022, March 7). LegalShield. https://www.legalshield.com/blog/landlord-tenant/four-reasons-evict-tenant/

5 Reasons Townhomes Are Good Investments for a First Rental Property. (2022, November 23). New Jersey Real Estate Network. https://www.newjerseyrealestatenetwork.com/blog/reasons-townhomes-make-good-first-rental-properties/

5 Reasons Why Real Estate Is a Stable Investment. (2022, December 28). DGY Investments. https://dgyinvestments.com/blog/5-reasons-why-real-estate-is-a-stable-investment/

5 Strategies for Reducing Operating Costs. (n.d.). Parcel Pending. https://www.parcelpending.com/en-us/blog/5-strategies-for-reducing-operating-costs/

5 Things You Should Know about the Fair Housing Act. (n.d.). State Property Management LLC. https://www.managecentralfloridaproperty.com/fair-housing-act.html

6 Tips to Successfully Showing a Rental Property. (2021, July 13). Bay Property Management Group. https://www.baymgmtgroup.com/blog/6-tips-successfully-show-rental-property/

7 Pros and Cons of Owning a Short Term Rental. (n.d.). Short Term Rental Manager. https://shorttermrentalmanager.com/7-pros-and-cons-of-owning-a-short-term-rental/

7 Reasons You Should Invest in a Mid-Term Rental. (2023, June 30). Semi-Retired MD. https://semiretiredmd.com/7-reasons-you-should-invest-in-a-mid-term-rental/

10 Common Tenant Complaints and How to Reach a Resolution. (n.d.). The Fitzgerald Law Firm. https://thefitzgeraldlawfirm.com/10-common-tenant-complaints-and-how-to-reach-a-resolution/

10 Creative Ways to Make Your Home Purchase Offer Stand Out. (2024). Mountain America Credit Union. https://www.macu.com/must-reads/mortgage/make-your-home-purchase-offer-stand-out-fined

10 Questions That Should Be on Every Rental Application. (2023, October 6). https://www.mysmartmove.com/blog/rental-application-questions

11 Ways Landlords Can Cut Costs & Save Money. (2020, April 23). Mashvisor. https://www.mashvisor.com/blog/ways-landlords-cut-costs-save-money/

Advantages and Disadvantages of Foreclosure Investments. (n.d.). Evergreen Investments. https://evergreeninvestments.co/blog/advantages-and-disadvantages-of-foreclosure-investments/

Airbnb. (n.d.). *How to Become a Superhost.* https://www.airbnb.com/help/article/829#section-heading-2-0

Airbnb Data on 37568 Vacation Rentals in Nashville, Tennessee. (n.d.). AirDNA. https://www.airdna.co/vacation-rental-data/app/us/tennessee/nashville/overview

Airbnb Service Fees—What You Need to Know. (n.d.). Intasure. https://intasure.com/blog/airbnb-service-fees-what-you-need-to-know/

Airbnb Virtual Assistant. (n.d.). Aristo Sourcing. https://aristosourcing.com/airbnb-virtual-assistant/

Airbnb Welcome Book: How to Create a Comprehensive Guide for Your Guests. (2023, December 20). iGMS. https://www.igms.com/airbnb-welcome-book/

AirDNA Data: Nashville. (n.d.) AirDNA. https://www.airdna.co/vacation-rental-data/app/us/tennessee/nashville/overview

Akin, J. (2022, March 21). *What Is Cash Offer Financing?* Experian. https://www.experian.com/blogs/ask-experian/what-is-cash-offer-financing/

Allred, C. (2023, November 2). *10 Real Estate Investment Exit Strategies to Consider.* Invest.net. https://invest.net/real-estate/exit-strategies#1_Sell

AmFam Team. (n.d.). *What Basic Landlord Forms Do You Need.* American Family Insurance. https://www.amfam.com/resources/articles/your-business/landlord-forms

Ancheta, A. (2024, February 7). *What Is a C Corp?* Investopedia. https://www.investopedia.com/terms/c/c-corporation.asp

An Introduction to Office Building Investing. (n.d.). Feldman Equities. https://www.feldmanequities.com/education/an-introduction-to-office-building-investing/

Araj, V. (n.d.). *Cash-Out Refinance: Rates and Guide for Homeowners.* https://www.rocketmortgage.com/learn/cash-out-refinance

Araj, V. (n.d.-b). *Lease Purchase Agreement: What You Should Know.* https://www.rocketmortgage.com/learn/lease-purchase-agreement

Araj, V. (n.d.-b). *How to Make an Offer on a House in 5 Steps.* https://www.rocketmortgage.com/learn/how-to-make-an-offer-on-a-house

Araj, V. (n.d.-d). *The Final Walkthrough: Checklist of What to Look For.* https://www.rocketmortgage.com/learn/a-complete-final-walkthrough-checklist#:~:text=The%20final%20walk%2Dthrough%20is%20your%20last%20opportunity%20to%20confirm,standards%20and%20include%20quality%20work.

Ates, K. (2024, January 12). *Normal Wear and Tear vs. Property Damage: A Landlord's Guide.* Rent Spree. https://www.rentspree.com/blog/normal-wear-and-tear#what-is-normal-wear-and-tear-

Ashworth, J. (2022, November 29). *The Beginner's Guide to Furnishing a Vacation Rental.* Lodgify. https://www.lodgify.com/blog/furnishing-vacation-rental/

Bank of America. (n.d.). *What Is a Home Equity Line of Credit and How Does it Work?* https://www.bankofamerica.com/mortgage/learn/what-is-a-home-equity-line-of-credit/

Beck, R. H. (2022, September 23). *What Is Commercial Real Estate?* Bankrate. https://www.bankrate.com/real-estate/commercial-real-estate/

Benefits of an LLC for Real Estate Investing – Blueprint Title. (2022, June 22). https://blueprinttitle.com/benefits-of-an-llc-for-real-estate-investing/

Bennett, J. (2022, August 27). *8 Crucial Tips for Hiring the Right Contractor for Your Remodel.* Better Homes & Gardens. https://www.bhg.com/home-improvement/advice/things-to-know-about-hiring-a-contractor/

Best Real Estate Investment Management Software. (n.d.). G2. https://www.g2.com/categories/real-estate-investment-management

Best Room & Home Rentals Experience. (n.d.). Bungalow. https://bungalow.com/arti cles/off-market-properties-what-are-they-and-how-to-buy

Best Ways to Communicate with Tenants: Email, Text, or Call? (n.d.). GoodDoors Property Management. https://www.gooddoors.com/tenant-communication

Bieber, C. (2023, December 7). *You Need Home Insurance Before Closing on a Home. Here's Why.* The Motley Fool. https://www.fool.com/the-ascent/insurance/ homeowners/articles/you-need-home-insurance-before-closing-on-a-home- heres-why/

Bitton, D. (2024, January 24). *Top 10 Real Estate Investor Software for Managing Rentals.* DoorLoop. https://www.doorloop.com/blog/real-estate-investor- software

Bmanassero. (2017, July 14). *10 Real Estate Investing Rules of Thumb Every Investor Should Know.* https://olddawgsreinetwork.com/real-estate-investing-rule-of- thumb/

Brauning, T., & Shemesh, J. (2022, February 16). *How to Detect Red Flags in Real Estate Investments.* Point Acquisitions. https://pointacquisitions.com/red-flag- in-real-estate/

Brock, M. (n.d.). *How to Find Real Estate Investors and Use Effective Investing Strategies.* https://www.rocketmortgage.com/learn/how-to-find-real-estate-investors

Bullock, M. (n.d.). *Everything You Need to Know About Your Security Deposit.* Apartments.com. https://www.apartments.com/blog/everything-you-need-to- know-about-your-security-deposit#:~:text=Generally%2C%20landlords% 20and%20property%20managers,ACH%20payment%20(electronic% 20payment)

Can I Use an S Corporation for Real Estate Investing. (n.d.). Nelson CPA. https://www. scorporationsexplained.com/s-corporation-for-real-estate-investing.htm

Carmody, B. (2023, December 8). *Best Tenant Screening Services of 2024.* Investopedia. https://www.investopedia.com/best-tenant-screening-services- 5070361#toc-best-for-realtors-smartmove

Cash for Keys: What It Is & What Landlords Should Know. (n.d.). Eaton Realty. https:// www.eatonrealty.com/blog/property-management/cash-keys-what-it-what- landlords-should-know

Cassell, W., Jr. (2023, May 28). *3 Reasons to Invest in Multi-Family Real Estate.* Investopedia. https://www.investopedia.com/articles/personal-finance/ 041216/3-reasons-invest-multifamily-real-estate.asp#:~:text=The%20Bot tom%20Line,-Much%20like%20stocks&text=There%20are%20many%20advan tages%20to,of%20hiring%20a%20property%20manager.

Ceizyk, D. (2023, August 17). *Investment Property Loans: What You Should Know.* LendingTree. https://www.lendingtree.com/home/mortgage/investment-prop erty-loans/#:~:text=You'll%20need%20a%20minimum,re%20buying%20a% 20multifamily%20home

CFI Team. (n.d.). *Annualized Rate of Return.* Corporate Finance Institute. https:// corporatefinanceinstitute.com/resources/wealth-management/annualized- rate-of-return/#:~:text=The%20annualized%20rate%20of%20return%20calcu lates%20the%20rate%20of%20return,the%20performance%20of%20different% 20investments

Charski, M. (2019, January). *How to Evaluate If Schools are Good in Your Neighbor- hood.* KeyBank. https://www.key.com/personal/financial-wellness/articles/ evaluate-schools-your-neighborhood.html#:~:text=Useful%20online%

20sources%20include%20GreatSchools,teacher%20ratio%2C%20and%20enrollment%20trends.

Chen, J. (2020, June 16). *Real Estate Owned (REO) Definition, Advantages, and Disadvantages.* Investopedia. https://www.investopedia.com/terms/r/realestateowned.asp

Chen, J. (2022, May 15). *Residential Rental Property Definition, Tax Pros & Cons.* Investopedia. https://www.investopedia.com/terms/r/residentialrentalproperty.asp

Co-hosting on Airbnb: Can You Do it Without Prior Hosting Experience? (n.d.). Shortterm Sage. https://shorttermsage.com/cohosting-on-airbnb-without-experience/

Collect Rent Online for Free. (n.d.). Apartments.com. https://www.apartments.com/rental-manager/online-rent-collection

Crace, M. (2024, February 29). *A Guide to Bank Statements for Your Mortgage.* Rocket Mortgage. https://www.rocketmortgage.com/learn/bank-statements#:~:text=You'll%20usually%20need%20to,qualify%20for%20your%20home%20loan

Crace, M. (2023, September 25). *Cap Rate: Defined and Explained.* Rocket Mortgage. https://www.rocketmortgage.com/learn/cap-rate

Dartiguenave, M. (2021, June 22). *Pros and Cons of Buying a Fixer-Upper.* Penrith Home Loans. https://www.penrithloans.com/2020/09/pros-and-cons-of-a-fixer-upper/

Decoding Home Buying: Identifying Hidden Red Flags When Buying a House. (n.d.). Pacific Keys Realty. https://pacifickeysrealty.com/blog/identifying-hidden-red-flags-when-buying-a-house

Davis, G. B. (n.d.). *6 Tips for Finding Off-Market Real Estate Properties.* R.E.Tipster. https://retipster.com/6-tips-for-finding-off-market-real-estate-properties/

Davis, G. B. (n.d.-b). *10 Real Estate Negotiation Tactics to Score the Best Deal Every Time.* R.E.Tipster. https://retipster.com/10-real-estate-negotiation-tactics-to-score-the-best-price-on-properties/#

Davis, G. B. (2022, November 28). *How Much Emergency Fund Should I Have as a Property Owner?* SparkRental. https://sparkrental.com/how-much-emergency-fund-should-i-have/

Dehan, A. (2024, January 24). *Buying a Fixer-Upper House: Pros and Cons.* Rocket Mortgage. https://www.rocketmortgage.com/learn/pros-cons-buying-fixer-upper-house

DeLoe, R. L., Esq. (2023, February 24). *18 Terms to Include in a Simple Lease Agreement.* Legalzoom. https://www.legalzoom.com/articles/18-terms-to-include-in-a-simple-lease-agreement

Dhir, R. (2023, December 30). *Negotiation: Definition, Stages, Skills, and Strategies.* Investopedia. https://www.investopedia.com/terms/n/negotiation.asp

Dickinson, G. (2023, November 28). *Wisconsin State Tax Guide: What You'll Pay in 2024.* AARP. https://states.aarp.org/wisconsin/state-taxes-guide

Dixon, A. (2023, December 12). *Determining How Much You Should Charge for Rent.* SmartAsset. https://smartasset.com/mortgage/how-much-you-should-charge-for-rent

Dixon, A. (2023, March 21). *Pros and Cons of Seller Financing (Updated).* SmartAsset. https://smartasset.com/mortgage/pros-and-cons-of-seller-financing

Domenick. (2020, January 17). *3 Ways a Nest Thermostat Benefits Landlords (No*

Common Wire Guide). Accidental Rental. https://accidentalrental.com/nest-thermostat-benefits/

Domenick. (2023, January 21). *5 Reasons to Install a Ring Video Doorbell in Your Rental (Instructions)*. Accidental Rental. https://accidentalrental.com/ring-video-doorbell-rental-instructions/

Donnelly, G. (2023, May 11). *How to Calculate Average Cash Flow on a Rental Property*. Honeycomb. https://honeycombinsurance.com/insurance-learning-center/average-cash-flow-on-rental-property/

Dow, N., & Veling, J. (2023, November 30). *Applying for a Loan Online vs. In Person: How to Choose*. NerdWallet. https://www.nerdwallet.com/article/loans/personal-loans/online-loan-or-bank-loan#:~:text=Many%20lenders%20with%20brick%2Dand,branch%20for%20in%2Dperson%20support

Due Diligence in Real Estate – What Is It, and Why Is It Important to Understand? (n.d.). The Orlando Law Group, PL. https://www.theorlandolawgroup.com/blog/all/due-diligence-in-real-estate/#:~:text=In%20real%20estate%2C%20due%20diligence,your%20homework%E2%80%9D%20prior%20to%20purchasing.

Dushey, P. (2023, November 17). *Navigating Commercial Real Estate's Post-Covid Transformation*. Forbes. https://www.forbes.com/sites/forbesbusinesscouncil/2023/11/17/navigating-commercial-real-estates-post-covid-transformation/?sh=3d56862214be

Eberlin, E. (2022, December 30). *A Checklist for Landlords with Tenants Moving Out*. The Balance. https://www.thebalancemoney.com/sample-move-out-checklist-for-landlords-and-tenants-2125000

Ellison, A. (2023, April 18). *What Does a Vacation Rental Property Manager Do?* AvantStay. https://avantstay.com/blog/what-does-a-property-manager-do/

Esajian, J.D. (n.d.). *Investing in Multifamily Real Estate: The Ultimate Guide*. Fortune-Builders. https://www.fortunebuilders.com/multifamily-investment-property/

Esajian, P. (n.d.). *Here's Why You Should Be Raw Land Investing*. FortuneBuilders. https://www.fortunebuilders.com/how-to-know-if-raw-land-investing-is-right-for-you/

Essential Negotiation Skills. (n.d.-b). MindTools. https://www.mindtools.com/aal02x7/essential-negotiation-skills

Feeney, C. (2023, February 19). *How to Find Investor-Friendly Realtors: Look for These 9 Skills*. HomeLight. https://www.homelight.com/blog/investor-friendly-realtors/

Fernando, J. (2024, January 26). *Internal Rate of Return (IRR): Formula and Examples*. Investopedia. https://www.investopedia.com/terms/i/irr.asp

Folger, J. (2024, February 23). *How to Calculate ROI on a Rental Property*. Investopedia. https://www.investopedia.com/articles/investing/062215/how-calculate-roi-rental-property.asp

Folger, J. (2024, February 27). *Rent-to-Own Homes: How the Process Works*. Investopedia. https://www.investopedia.com/updates/rent-to-own-homes/

Fontinelle, A. (2023, February 16). *Lease Purchase Agreement: Benefits for Buyers and Owners*. Forbes. https://www.forbes.com/advisor/mortgages/lease-purchase-agreement/

Formigle, I. (n.d.). *Real Estate Cycle: Riding the Ups & Downs of the Market*. Crowd-Street. https://www.crowdstreet.com/resources/investment-fundamentals/real-estate-cycle-phases

Fortune, A. (2023, June 29). *18 Ways to Get Your Offer Accepted & Win a Bidding War*.

Great Colorado Homes. https://greatcoloradohomes.com/blog/how-to-get-your-real-estate-offer-accepted-in-a-sellers-market.html

Franklin, J. B. (2024, January 2). *Real Estate Comps and How to Find Them.* Bankrate. https://www.bankrate.com/real-estate/how-to-find-real-estate-comps/

Freeze, P. (2023, January 20). *Top 5 Things to Emphasize in Your Tenant Welcome Packet.* Bay Property Management Group. https://www.baymgmtgroup.com/blog/top-5-things-emphasize-tenant-welcome-packet/

Fulmer, J. (n.d.). *Using Direct Mail Marketing to Find Off-Market Real Estate Deals.* Upright. https://learn.upright.us/real-estate-investing-blog/direct-mail-to-find-off-market-real-estate-deals#:~:text=You%20can%20definitely%20find%20great,including%20direct%20mail%2C%20is%20consistency

Graham, K. (2024, January 17). *How to Calculate Your Monthly Mortgage Payment: A Guide.* Rocket Mortgage. https://www.rocketmortgage.com/learn/how-to-calculate-mortgage

Guesty Marketing Team. (2024, January 14). *Everything You Need to Know about Airbnb's Host-Only Fee.* https://www.guesty.com/blog/everything-about-airbnb-host-only-fee/

Hall, J. (2023, February 21). *Move-in Checklist: A Guide for Landlords and Tenants.* Redfin. https://www.redfin.com/blog/move-in-checklist/

Hamann, J. (2023, November 27). *What Are the Pros and Cons of Owning an Apartment Complex?* Janover Multifamily Loans. https://www.multifamily.loans/apartment-finance-blog/what-are-the-pros-and-cons-of-owning-an-apartment-complex/

Hand, B. (2022, January 25). *What Is a Rent Grace Period, and How Does It Work?* Landing. https://www.hellolanding.com/blog/what-is-a-rent-grace-period-and-how-does-it-work/

Harbour, S. (2023, August 29). *The Landlord Life: 7 Tips to Save for Your First Rental Property.* Synchrony. https://www.synchronybank.com/blog/tips-to-save-for-rental-property/

Hare, D. (2023, April 19). *10 Benefits of Owning Land (2023).* APXN Property. https://apxnproperty.com/benefits-owning-land/

Hargrave, M. (2023, December 15). *Average Return: Meaning, Calculations and Examples.* Investopedia. https://www.investopedia.com/terms/a/averagereturn.asp#:~:text=Average%20Return%20Example&text=For%20instance%2C%20suppose%20an%20investment,and%20then%20divided%20by%205

Hargrave, M. (2021, March 22). *Price-to-Rent Ratio: Determining If It's Better to Buy or Rent.* Investopedia. https://www.investopedia.com/terms/p/price-to-rent-ratio.asp#:~:text=The%20price%2Dto%2Drent%20ratio%20is%20the%20ratio%20of%20home,valued%2C%20or%20in%20a%20bubble.

Hatzenbihler, E. (2023, April 19). *Should You Hire a Property Manager or Do It Yourself?* Avail. https://www.avail.co/education/articles/should-you-hire-a-property-manager-or-do-it-yourself

Haug, D. (2020, August 7). *Investing in Commercial Real Estate, the Pros and Cons.* Lighthouse Commercial Real Estate. https://www.lighthousecre.com/invest/investing-in-commercial-real-estate/

Have You Thought of Mid-Term Rentals? Here's What You Should Know. (2023, February 2). Kiavi. https://www.kiavi.com/blog/have-you-thought-of-mid-term-rentals-heres-what-you-should-know

Hayes, A. (2023, March 20). *Exit Strategy Definition for an Investment or Business.* Investopedia. https://www.investopedia.com/terms/e/exitstrategy.asp

Hennigan, L. & Bottorff. (2022, December 27). *What is Bookkeeping? Everything You Need to Know*. Forbes. https://www.forbes.com/advisor/business/what-is-bookkeeping/

Henson, T. (2023, March 14). *Top 7 Tips for Networking in Real Estate*. Beach Front Property Management Inc. https://bfpminc.com/top-7-tips-for-networking-in-real-estate/

Hepworth, A. (2024, February 20). *19 Rental Sites like Airbnb, Ranked for 2024*. Pure-Wow. https://www.purewow.com/travel/sites-like-airbnb

Higuera, V. (2024, January 12). *Conventional Loan Requirements 2024 | First-Time Home Buyer*. The Mortgage Reports. https://themortgagereports.com/95024/conventional-loan-requirements

Homer Hoyt: An Introduction. (2019, January 29). Hoyt Group. https://hoytgroup.org/wp-content/uploads/2019/03/Homer-Hoyt-Bio-Grant-and-Steve-Final-1-29-2019.pd

How Do You Calculate Annual Growth Rates? (n.d.). FutureLearn. https://www.future learn.com/info/courses/introduction-to-environmental-science/0/steps/270677#:~:text=Population%20Growth%20Calculation,10%20years)%20was%2012%25

How Much Do Property Managers Charge? (2021, October 19). Hospitable. https://hospitable.com/how-much-property-managers-charge/

How Much Should I Charge for My Airbnb? (n.d.). Uplisting. https://www.uplisting.io/blog/how-much-should-i-charge-for-my-airbnb

How Much Should I Charge for Rent? (2021, February 14). Zillow. https://www.zillow.com/rental-manager/resources/how-much-can-i-rent-my-house-for/

How to Prepare a House for Rental. (n.d.). Eaton Realty. https://www.eatonrealty.com/blog/property-management/how-prepare-house-rental

How to Take Great Airbnb Photos: An Essential Guide. (2024, January 30). iGMS. https://www.igms.com/airbnb-photos/

Hubspina, M. (2024, January 12). *Completing Move-In Inspections: Tips Landlords Should Know*. DoorLoop. https://www.doorloop.com/blog/landlord-tips-for-move-in-inspections

Hugh's Media Blog. (n.d.). *Why Investing in Commercial Office Space Beats Investing in a Home*. Greetly. https://www.greetly.com/press/why-investing-in-commercial-office-space-is-better-than-investing-in-a-home

Hughes, E. (n.d.). *Do Condos Make Good Rental Properties?* Rental Income Advisors. https://www.rentalincomeadvisors.com/blog/do-condos-make-good-rental-properties

Is a Smart Thermostat Worth Buying? (n.d.). Efficiency Vermont.

Investopedia Team. (2023, April 8). *Landlord: Duties, Responsibilities, and Rights*. Investopedia. https://www.investopedia.com/terms/l/landlord.asp https://www.efficiencyvermont.com/blog/how-to/is-a-smart-thermostat-worth-buying

Jackson, K. (2023, August 4). *9 Common Tenant Complaints (and How Landlords Can Resolve Them*. Avail. https://www.avail.co/education/articles/common-tenant-complaints

Jankelow, L. (2022, October 3). *Approve and Reject Tenants the Right Way*. Avail. https://www.avail.co/education/articles/approving-tenants-the-right-way#:~:text=You%20can%2C%20however%2C%20reject%20tenants,to%20why%20you%20rejected%20them

Jankowitz, S. (2023, February 1). *8 Red Flags to Look Out for When Buying an Invest-ment Property*. Cambridge Real Estate. https://www.cambridgesage.com/blog/investment-red-flags

Johnston, E. (n.d.). *How to Calculate Before Tax Cash Flows*. Chron.com. https://smallbusiness.chron.com/calculate-before-tax-cash-flows-17499.html

Jozsa, E. (2023, February 19). *The Pros and Cons of Multifamily Investing*. Janover Multifamily Loans. https://www.multifamily.loans/apartment-finance-blog/the-pros-and-cons-of-multifamily-investing/

Kagan, J. (2023, November 5). *What Is an S Corp? Definition, Taxes, and How to File*. Investopedia. https://www.investopedia.com/terms/s/subchapters.asp

Kasch, A. (2022, January 3). *How Unlicensed Contractors Can Cost You*. Angi. https://www.angi.com/articles/how-unlicensed-contractors-can-cost-you.htm

Keel, A. (2023, August 17). *The Pros and Cons of Mobile Home Park Investing*. Forbes. https://www.forbes.com/sites/forbesbusinesscouncil/2023/08/17/the-pros-and-cons-of-mobile-home-park-investing/?sh=15e938e86569

Kemmis, S. (2024, January 6). *Why 'Bleisure' Travel Gives Short-Term Rentals like Airbnb a Boost over Hotels*. The Post-Journal. https://www.post-journal.com/news/business/2024/01/why-bleisure-travel-gives-short-term-rentals-like-airbnb-a-boost-over-hotels/

Kenton, W. (2024, January 29). *Net Operating Income (NOI): Definition, Calculation, Components, and Example*. Investopedia. https://www.investopedia.com/terms/n/noi.asp#:~:text=How%20to%20Calculate%20Net%20Operating,laundry%20machines%2C%20and%20so%20on.

Kielar, H. (2024, March 4). *What Is a Conventional Loan?* Rocket Mortgage. https://www.rocketmortgage.com/learn/conventional-mortgage

Kilroy, A. (2024, February 6). *Tax Benefits of Real Estate Investing*. SmartAsset. https://smartasset.com/taxes/tax-benefits-of-real-estate-investing

Kimmons, J. (2018, November 21). *How to Calculate Investor Cash Flow Before Taxes (CFBT)*. The Balance. https://www.thebalancemoney.com/how-to-calculate-investor-cash-flow-before-taxes-cfbt-2866788

Kurby Team. (2023, April 30). *How to Create an Effective Maintenance Request System*. Kurby Real Estate. https://blog.kurby.ai/how-to-create-an-effective-maintenance-request-system/#key_components_of_an_effective_maintenance_request_system

Lake, R. (2022, November 16). *What Is the IRR for Real Estate Investments?* Smart Asset. https://smartasset.com/investing/internal-rate-of-return-real-estate-investments

How to Choose the Best Location for Investment Property. (2022, December 14). Mashvisor. https://www.mashvisor.com/blog/best-location-for-investment-property/#six-qualities-that-make-a-city-or-neighborhood-great-for-investment-property

Lee, C. (2022, November 7). *Should You List a Rental on Zillow?* Landlord Gurus. https://landlordgurus.com/should-list-a-rental-on-zillow/

Ligon, M. (2023, March 3). *A Real Estate Investor's Guide to Investing in Vacant Land*. Forbes. https://www.forbes.com/sites/forbesbusinesscouncil/2023/03/03/a-real-estate-investors-guide-to-investing-in-vacant-land/?sh=55e99651f321

Lindquist, S. (2022, February 8). *14 Essential Questions to Ask a Contractor before Hiring*. Asher Lasting Exteriors. https://goasher.com/home-improvement/questions-to-ask-a-contractor/

Long-Term vs. Short-Term Real Estate Investment: Which Is Right for You. (2023, July 28). The Greens. https://thegreensgh.com/long-term-vs-short-term-real-estate-investment-which-is-right-for-you/

Lucas, T. (2024, January 1). *How to Cash-Out Refinance Investment Property: 2024 Guidelines.* The Mortgage Reports. https://themortgagereports.com/25521/cash-out-refinance-rental-property-guidelines-mortgage-rates

Luxon, B. (2021, August 6). *How to Get Great Rental Photos for Your Listing.* LandlordStudio. https://www.landlordstudio.com/blog/how-to-get-perfect-rental-photography

Luxon, B. (2023, December 13). *The Best Way to Collect Rent Payments from Your Tenants.* LandlordStudio. https://www.landlordstudio.com/blog/the-best-way-to-collect-rent-from-your-tenants

Mancini, J. (2023, April 4). *Are You Budgeting Enough CapEx for Your Investment Property?* Yahoo. https://finance.yahoo.com/news/budgeting-enough-capex-investment-property-204855305.html#:~:text=There%20are%20some%20gen eral%20guidelines,or%20renovations%20as%20they%20arise.

Marcek, S. (2022, May 13). *Refunding Security Deposits: Everything You Need to Know* PayRent. https://www.payrent.com/articles/refunding-security-deposits-everything-you-need-to-know/

Martin, A. (2024, February 28). *Owner Financing: What It Is and How It Works.* Bankrate. https://www.bankrate.com/mortgages/owner-financing/

Maxwell, T. (2023, July 12). *How Long Does a Mortgage Preapproval Letter Last?* Experian. https://www.experian.com/blogs/ask-experian/how-long-does-a-mortgage-preapproval-last/#:~:text=Most%20preapprovals%20are%20good%20for,you%20begin%20serious%20house%20hunting

McCann, K. (2024, February 8). *Mid-Term Rentals: Pros and Cons for Property Owners.* Azibo. https://www.azibo.com/blog/mid-term-rentals-pros-and-cons-for-property-owners

McCracken, M. (2022, October 17). *Most Common Tenant Complaints and How to Handle Them.* Bay Property Management Group. https://www.baymgmtgroup.com/blog/common-tenant-complaints/

McCracken, M. (2021, December 6). *What Is Rental Property Investment?* Bay Property Management Group. https://www.baymgmtgroup.com/blog/what-is-rental-property-investment/

Merrill, T. (n.d.). *Are Condos a Good Investment? The Pros & Cons in 2023.* FortuneBuilders. https://www.fortunebuilders.com/the-pros-and-cons-of-condo-investing/

Merrill, T. (n.d.). *The Best Exit Strategies for Real Estate.* FortuneBuilders. https://www.fortunebuilders.com/real-estate-exit-strategies-part-1/

Meyer, S. (2023, September 7). *Everything You Need to Know about Due Diligence in Real Estate.* The Zebra. https://www.thezebra.com/resources/home/due-dili gence-real-estate/

Miller, K. (2020, July 20). *The Lease Signing Process for Landlords and Tenants.* Rentec Direct. https://www.rentecdirect.com/blog/lease-signing-process/#:~:text=Owner%20or%20manager%20sends%20an,offer%20to%20rent%20the%20prop erty.

Miller, K. (2018, November 18). *Pros and Cons of a Fixed-Term Lease versus a Month-to-Month Lease.* Rentec Direct. https://www.rentecdirect.com/blog/fixed-term-lease-versus-month-to-month/

Morby, P. (2023, April 5). *From Survival to Success: The Power of Creative Financing in Uncertain Times.* Forbes. https://www.forbes.com/sites/forbesbusinesscouncil/2023/04/05/from-survival-to-success-the-power-of-creative-financing-in-uncertain-times/?sh=20fab87a7ea1

Mordkovich, B. (n.d.). *How Much Does It Cost to Furnish & Setup a New Airbnb.* BuildYourBnB. https://www.buildyourbnb.com/blog-post/how-much-does-it-cost-to-furnish-setup-a-new-airbnb

Mueller, J. (2024, February 6). *Should You Set Up an S Corporation for Your Real Estate Investment?* James Moore. https://www.jmco.com/articles/real-estate/s-corporation-for-real-estate-investment/

Murdock, C. (2019, April 9). *Tenant Screening Questions to Ask Rental Applicants.* RentSpree. https://www.rentspree.com/blog/tenant-screening-questions

Nelson, J. (2023, June 24). *Real Estate Investing: How to Find a Partner for Your Business Plan.* Forbes. https://www.forbes.com/sites/jamesnelson/2023/06/24/real-estate-investing-how-to-find-a-partner-for-your-business-plan/?sh=64cc4ef33638

Nesbit, J. (2023, April 3). *How to Run a Tenant Background Check.* U.S. News & World Report. https://realestate.usnews.com/real-estate/articles/how-to-run-a-tenant-background-check

Nesbit, J. *What Is a Month-to-Month Lease?* (2023, June 28). U.S. News & World Report. https://realestate.usnews.com/real-estate/articles/what-is-a-month-to-month-lease#:~:text=A%20month%2Dto%2Dmonth%20lease%20is%20a%20rental%20agreement%20with,or%20landlord%20terminates%20the%20contract

Nic. (2024, February 4). *How to Do Creative Financing in Real Estate: 10 Best Tips.* Nic's Guide. https://nicsguide.com/how-to-do-creative-financing

Odoardi, R. (n.d.). *What Is a Land Lease?* Blue Water Mortgage. https://bluewatermtg.com/what-is-a-ground-lease/

Orr, J. (n.d.). *Real Estate Investing Rules of Thumb.* Real Estate Financial Planner. https://realestatefinancialplanner.com/real-estate-investing-rules-of-thumb/

Orr, J. (n.d.). *The Ultimate Guide to Real Estate Appreciation.* Real Estate Financial Planner. https://realestatefinancialplanner.com/appreciation/#

Owner Carryback Mortgages. (n.d.). LegalMatch Law Library. https://www.legalmatch.com/law-library/article/owner-carryback-mortgages.html

Park, G. (2023, September 9). *Should You Hire a Property Management Company?* liv. https://liv.rent/blog/landlords/should-you-hire-a-property-management-company/#Do_you_need_to_hire_a_property_management_company

Petry, M. (2023, December 7). *What Is a Single-Family Home?* Bankrate. https://www.bankrate.com/real-estate/what-is-a-single-family-home/#what-is

Portfolio Loan. (n.d.). North American Savings Bank. https://www.nasb.com/lending/solutions/non-qm-loans/portfolio-loan#:~:text=A%20portfolio%20loan%20is%20a,to%20help%20the%20local%20community.

Price-to-Rent Ratio in the 50 Largest U.S. Cities – 2022 Edition. (2022, June 1). SmartAsset. https://smartasset.com/data-studies/price-to-rent-ratio-in-the-50-largest-us-cities-2022

Property Investor Insurance: What Coverage Do You Need. (2023, May 16). LandesBlosch. https://www.landesblosch.com/blog/property-investor-insurance-what-coverage-do-you-need

Pros and Cons of Investing in Retail Spaces. (2023, May 9). 99acres. https://www.

99acres.com/articles/pros-and-cons-of-investing-in-retail-spaces.html

Rawson, C. (2023, August 18). *What Does Superhost Mean on Airbnb?* NerdWallet. https://www.nerdwallet.com/article/travel/what-does-superhost-mean-on-airbnb

Real Estate Fund Management Software. (n.d.). SyndicationPro. https://syndicationpro.com/real-estate-investment-management-software

Real Estate Lawyer Information: When Should I Retain a Lawyer? (n.d.). Morgan & Morgan. https://www.forthepeople.com/practice-areas/business-litigation-lawyers/real-estate/when-should-i-retain-lawyer/#:~:text=Leasing%2FRenting%20Property%3A%20If%20you,prevent%20any%20future%20legal%20problems.

Reasons for Rent Due Date Extensions. (n.d.). FasterCapital. https://fastercapital.com/topics/reasons-for-rent-due-date-extensions.html

Rentometer: House and Apartment Rental Rate Comps. (n.d.). Rentometer. https://www.rentometer.com/analysis/2-bed/2201-west-end-ave-nashville-tn/uknmWP6lJcA/quickview

Reuther, K. (n.d.). *Structuring Your Rental Business: LLC vs C Corp vs S Corp.* Turbo-Tenant. https://www.turbotenant.com/blog/structuring-your-rental-business-llc-vs-c-corp-vs-s-corp/

Richardson, S. (2024, February 2). *Foreclosure Defined: What It Is, How to Avoid It, and What It Means to You.* Rocket Mortgage.

Rizek, E. (2019, November 10). *Investment Property for Sale: Local vs Non-Local.* Mashvisor. https://www.mashvisor.com/blog/investment-property-for-sale-local-non-local/amp/

Rohde, J. (2022, August 3). *How to Run a Neighborhood Analysis for Real Estate Investing.* Roofstock. https://learn.roofstock.com/blog/neighborhood-analysis

Rohde, J. (2022, May 30). *How to Vet and Find Investor-Friendly Lenders in 2022.* Roofstock. https://learn.roofstock.com/blog/investor-friendly-lenders https://www.rocketmortgage.com/learn/foreclosure-definition

Rohde, J. (n.d.). *Landlord Studio vs. Apartments.com (Cozy): 2024 Comparison.* Stessa. https://www.stessa.com/blog/landlord-studio-vs-apartments-cozy/

Rohde, J. (2022, February 12). *The Pros and Cons of a Buy-and-Hold Real Estate Strategy.* Roofstock. https://learn.roofstock.com/blog/buy-and-hold-real-estate

Rohde, J. (n.d.). *What to Do When You Get a Partial Rent Payment from a Tenant.* Stessa. https://www.stessa.com/blog/partial-rent/

Rohde, J. (n.d.). *Which Expenses Are Operating Expenses for Rental Property?* Stessa. https://www.stessa.com/blog/operating-expenses-rental-property/#:~:text=Operating%20expenses%20are%20the%20recurring,%2C%20insurance%2C%20and%20property%20taxes

Sanders, K. (2023, April 27). *How to Hire and Manage a Contractor Checklist and Tips.* The Spruce. https://www.thespruce.com/hiring-and-managing-home-repair-contractor-1825128

Scaling Your Real Estate Investment Portfolio. (2023, July 22). Turnkey Invest Properties. https://turnkeyinvestproperties.com/scaling-your-real-estate-investment-portfolio/

Scalisi, T. (2023, June 8). *20 Types of Contractors in Construction.* Levelset. https://www.levelset.com/blog/types-of-contractors/#7_Electrical

S Corporations. (n.d.). Internal Revenue Service. https://www.irs.gov/businesses/small-businesses-self-employed/s-corporations#:~:text=S%20corporations%

20are%20corporations%20that,shareholders%20for%20federal%20tax%20pur
poses.

See, J. (2024, January 22). *Factors That Impact Your Cost of Homeowners Insurance.*
Bankrate. https://www.bankrate.com/insurance/homeowners-insurance/
factors-that-impact-home-insurance-rates/#factors-that-impact-your-home-
insurance-rate

Segal, T. (2024, February 27). *Guide to Closing on a House: What to Expect during the
Closing Process.* Bankrate. https://www.bankrate.com/mortgages/understand
ing-the-closing-process/#closing-costs

Segal, T. (2023, November 21). *Portfolio Mortgages: What They Are and How They
Work.* Bankrate. https://www.bankrate.com/mortgages/portfolio-loan/#what-
is

Segal, T. (2023, August 29). *What Is Real Estate Wholesaling? How It Works, Example,
and Strategies.* Investopedia. https://www.investopedia.com/ask/answers/
100214/what-goal-real-estate-wholesaling.asp#:~:text=In%20real%20estate%
20wholesaling%2C%20a,seller%20and%20keeps%20the%20difference

Segoviano, A. (2022, July 27). *Move-Out Inspection Basics for Landlords and Tenants.*
Avail. https://www.avail.co/education/articles/move-out-inspection-basics-
for-landlords-and-tenants

Semrush Team. (2023, June 26). *Airbnb SEO: 12 Tips to Boost Your Listing's Visibility.*
Semrush Blog. https://www.semrush.com/blog/airbnb-seo/?
kw=&cmp=US_SRCH_DSA_Blog_EN&label=dsa_pagefeed&Net-
work=g&Device=c&utm_content=683861103836&kwid=dsa-
2263819780519&cmpid=18348486859&ag-
pid=156312208213&BU=Core&extid=97592268616&adpos=&gad_-
source=1&gclid=CjwKCAiAuYuvBhApEiwAzq_YiWjNPxhkVAxMmdG4-
Xarwjy5L_1n_a0XnXfiWxdgq3Qe__gkKSAC2xoChKgQAvD_BwE

The Best ROI Amenities for your Airbnb Vacation Rental. (n.d.). Hostaway.
https://www.hostaway.com/blog/the-best-roi-amenities-for-your-airbnb-
vacation-rental/

Serhant, R. (2022, January 13). *9 Things a Good Real Estate Agent Should Do for You.*
Forbes. https://www.forbes.com/sites/ryanserhant/2022/01/13/9-things-a-
good-real-estate-agent-should-do-for-you/?sh=3ed5bc0a6786

Sharkey, S. (n.d.). *Property Taxes: What They Are and How to Calculate Them.* Rocket
Mortgage. https://www.rocketmortgage.com/learn/property-tax

Shewale, R. (2024, January 15). *Facebook Statistics & Trends to Know in 2024.*
DemandSage. https://www.demandsage.com/facebook-statistics/#:~:text=
How%20many%20people%20use%20Facebook,of%20billion%20daily%20ac
tive%20users.

Shonk, K. (2024, January 12). *Top 10 Negotiation Skills You Must Learn to Succeed.*
Program on Negotiation at Harvard Law School. https://www.pon.harvard.
edu/daily/negotiation-skills-daily/top-10-negotiation-skills/

Short-Term vs Long-Term Rentals. (n.d.). McCaw Property Management. https://
mccawpropertymanagement.com/short-term-vs-long-term-rentals/

Singh, J. (n.d.). *Managing Multiple Rental Properties: Tips for Success.* Steadily.
https://www.steadily.com/blog/managing-multiple-rental-properties-tips-
for-success#:~:text=Establishing%20a%20structured%20system%20-
for,pace%20with%20your%20expanding%20operations.

Smith, L. (2023, August 17). *How to Increase Your Real Estate Net Worth with Lever-*

aging. Investopedia. https://www.investopedia.com/articles/mortgages-real-estate/10/increase-your-real-estate-net-worth.asp#:~:text=Leverage%20uses%20borrowed%20capital%20or,to%20losses%20if%20values%20decline.

Snyder, K and Main, K. (2022, August 15). *Real Estate LLC Guide: Pros, Cons & How to Set Up*. Forbes. https://www.forbes.com/advisor/business/real-estate-llc-guide/

Steinberg, S. (2024, January 21). *Seller Financing: How It Works, Pros and Cons and If It's a Good Idea*. Rocket Mortgage. https://www.rocketmortgage.com/learn/seller-financing

Stevens, R. (2022, April 20). *How to Find Vacancy Rate in Any Area*. New Silver. https://newsilver.com/the-lender/how-to-find-vacancy-rate/

Struyk, T. (2023, June 7). *The Factors of a "Good" Location*. Investopedia. https://www.investopedia.com/financial-edge/0410/the-5-factors-of-a-good-location.aspx

Simplified Pricing. (n.d.). Airbnb. https://www.airbnb.ie/e/commissione-semplifi-cata-guida#:~:text=From%20December%202020%2C%20Simplified%20Pricing,Bahamas%2C%20Argentina%20and%20Taiwan)

Successfully Transitioning a Rental Property between Tenants. (2023, May 11). Harris-burg Property Management Group. https://www.564rent.com/blog/how-to-transition-a-rental-property-between-tenants

Sutton, G., Esq. (2015, January 8). *Why You Should Never Hold Real Estate in a C Corp*. Corporate Direct. https://corporatedirect.com/c-corps-s-corps/why-you-should-never-hold-real-estate-in-a-c-corporation/

Sutton, T. (n.d.). *What Is Cash Flow in Real Estate? How to Maximize Cash Flow at Your Property*. ButterflyMX. https://butterflymx.com/blog/cash-flow-real-estate/

Tejada, V. (2023, August 15). *Real Estate Appreciation: Comparing Natural vs. Forced*. Azibo. https://www.azibo.com/blog/real-estate-appreciation#:~:text=Natural%20appreciation%20refers%20to%20the,renovations%20or%20increas ing%20rental%20income

The Advantages and Risks of 1031 Exchanges. (n.d.). Innago. https://innago.com/the-advantages-and-risks-of-1031-exchanges/

The Four Returns in Real Estate Investing: Cash Flow Is NOT Everything. (2019, November 27). REICO. https://denverinvestmentrealestate.com/the-four-returns-real-estate-cash-flow-not-everything/

The Importance of Job Growth in Real Estate Investments. (2023, June 15). Penn Capital. https://www.linkedin.com/pulse/importance-job-growth-real-estate-investments-penn-capital

The Pros and Cons of Keyless Entry Systems in Rental Properties. (2022, November 3). Bay Property Management Group. https://www.baymgmtgroup.com/blog/pros-cons-keyless-entry-systems-rental-properties/

The Pros and Cons of Purchasing a Rental Property with Cash. (2021, August 17). Bay Property Management Group. https://www.baymgmtgroup.com/blog/pros-and-cons-purchasing-rental-property-with-cash/

Tips to Build a Long-Term Real Estate Investment Strategy. (n.d.). RCN Capital. https://rcncapital.com/blog/tips-to-build-a-long-term-real-estate-invest ment-strategy

Tolentino, R. (n.d.). *What Is a Mobile Home Park?* R.E.Tipster. https://retipster.com/terms/mobile-home-park/

Tom. (2023, December 11). *Check-Out Instructions for Airbnb: A Guide to a Smooth*

Departure. Host Tools. https://hosttools.com/blog/short-term-rental-tips/airbnb-check-out-instructions/#t-1702313456731

Torres. J. (2023, August 9). *Uncovering the Real Estate Cycle: 4 Stages of Investing.* Swiftlane. https://swiftlane.com/blog/uncovering-the-real-estate-cycle-4-stages-of-investing/

Townhouse Construction Surged in 2021. (2022, February 21). National Association of Home Builders. https://www.nahb.org/blog/2022/02/townhouse-construction-surged-in-2021/

Tross, K. (2023, May 8). *The 6 Types of Commercial Real Estate Property.* VTS. https://www.vts.com/blog/the-6-types-of-commercial-real-estate-properties

Tzanetos, G. (2022, October 31). *Getting a Mortgage vs. Paying Cash: What's the Difference?* Investopedia. https://www.investopedia.com/articles/investing/111116/getting-mortgage-vs-paying-cash-investment-properties.asp

Umbrasas, K. (2019, November 26). *Real Estate Comps: How to Find Comparables for Real Estate.* Zillow. https://www.zillow.com/learn/real-estate-comps/

Van Eyk, L. (2023, April 28). *A Landlord's Guide to Mid-Term Rentals.* Steadily. https://www.steadily.com/blog/guide-to-mid-term-rentals

Van Eyk, L. (2024, January 10). *Are Townhomes a Good Investment in 2024?* Steadily. https://www.steadily.com/blog/are-townhomes-a-good-investment

Waller, R. (2024, January 18). *House Hacking – Pros & Cons (2024).* Guelph Realtors. https://bethandryan.ca/house-hacking-pros-and-cons/

What Are the Benefits of Hiring a handyman. (n.d.). American Home Protect. American Home Protect. https://americanhomeprotectllc.com/benefits-of-hiring-handyman-services#:~:text=Hiring%20a%20handyman%20-can%20save,tasks%20that%20homeowners%20may%20need

What Does Due Diligence Mean for a Homebuyer? (2023, September 18). Showcase Properties of Central Florida. https://www.showcaseocala.com/homebuyer-due-diligence/

What Does Off-Market Mean in Real Estate Listing? (n.d.). Florida Realty Marketplace. https://www.floridarealtymarketplace.com/blog/what-does-off-market-mean-in-real-estate-listing.html

What Happens After You Make an Offer? (2018, October). Atlantic Bay Mortgage Group. https://www.atlanticbay.com/knowledge-center/what-happens-after-you-make-an-offer

What Is a Buy Box? (n.d.). Investor Loan Source. https://ils.cash/what-is-a-buy-box/

What Is a Cash on Cash Return? (n.d.). Reliant Real Estate Management. https://www.reliant-mgmt.com/real-estate/cash-on-cash-return

What Is a Loan-to-Value Ratio and How Does It Relate to My Costs? (2020, September 9). Consumer Financial Protection Bureau. https://www.consumerfinance.gov/ask-cfpb/what-is-a-loan-to-value-ratio-and-how-does-it-relate-to-my-costs-en-121/#:~:text=The%20loan%2Dto%2Dvalue%20(,will%20require%20private%20mortgage%20insurance

What Is Earnest Money & How Much You Should Pay. (n.d.). Chase Bank. https://www.chase.com/personal/mortgage/education/financing-a-home/understanding-earnest-money

What Is Multifamily Housing and What Are the Benefits? (2023, March 30). Property Inspect. https://propertyinspect.com/blog/what-is-multifamily-housing-and-benefits/

Why Airbnb Reviews Are Critical & How to Get More of Them. (n.d.). Uplisting. https://www.uplisting.io/blog/why-airbnb-reviews-are-critical-how-to-get-more-of-them

Wichter, Z. (2021, February 2). *How to Make Your Home Offer Stand Out.* Bankrate. https://www.bankrate.com/real-estate/ways-to-make-home-offer-stand-out/

Wood, K., & Getler, T. (2024, January 22). *Cash-Out Refinance: How It Works and What to Know.* NerdWallet. https://www.nerdwallet.com/article/mortgages/refinance-cash-out

Woodman, C. (2023, May 24). *How to Scale Your Real Estate Portfolio.* New Silver. https://newsilver.com/the-lender/how-to-scale-your-real-estate-portfolio/

Wright, R. G. (2020, November 25). *What Is a Typical Emergency Fund in Real Estate?* The Investor's Edge. https://www.theinvestorsedge.com/blog/what-is-a-typical-emergency-fund-in-real-estate#:~:text=There%20are%20two%20types%20of,5%25%20for%20capital%20improvements)

Writing a Real Estate Offer Letter: 9 Things to Include. (2019, August 1). Mashvisor. https://www.mashvisor.com/blog/writing-real-estate-offer-letter-things-include/

Made in the USA
Columbia, SC
10 September 2024

42058013R00119